GraphicScience Biographies

Avicenna and the Book of Medicine

Jordi Bayarri

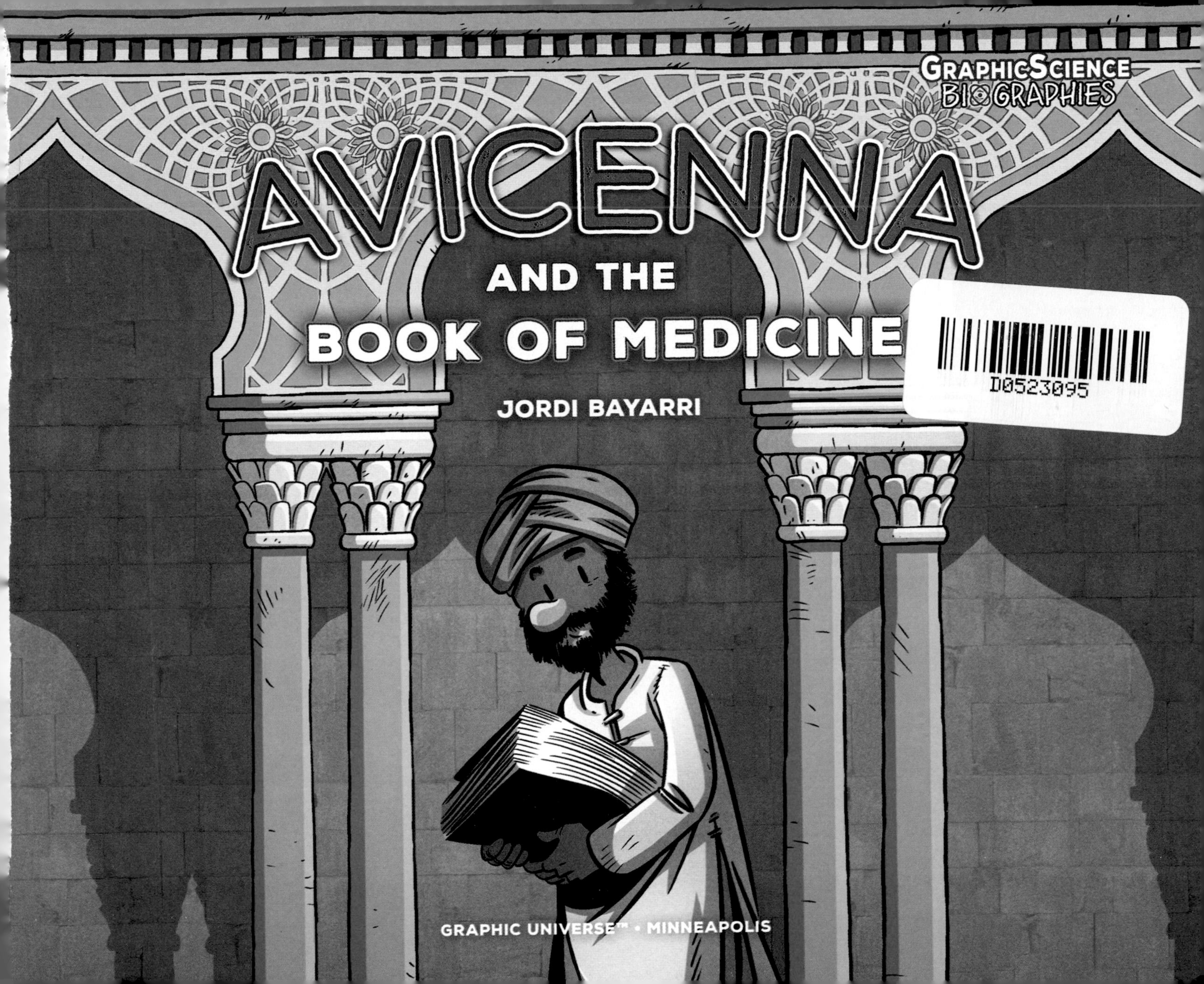

Graphic Universe™ • Minneapolis

Story and art by Jordi Bayarri
Historical and scientific consultation by Dr. Tayra M. C. Lanuza-Navarro, PhD in History of Science
Translated from the Spanish text by Zab Translation
Coloring by Dani Seijas
Coloring assistance by Mr. Jav! Doodles

Copyright © 2022 by Jordi Bayarri
Avicena, el canon de la medicina © by Colección Científicos
First American edition published in 2023 by Graphic Universe™

Graphic Universe™ is a trademark of Lerner Publishing Group, Inc.

Graphic Universe™
An imprint of Lerner Publishing Group, Inc.
241 First Avenue North
Minneapolis, MN 55401 USA

For reading levels and more information, look up this title at www.lernerbooks.com.

Image credit: Page 37: Portrait of Avicenna provided by Everett Collection Inc/Alamy Stock Photo.

Main body text set in CCDaveGibbonsLower.
Typeface provided by Comicraft.

Library of Congress Cataloging-in-Publication Data

Names: Bayarri, Jordi, 1972– author, illustrator.
Title: Avicenna and the book of medicine / Jordi Bayarri ; translated from the Spanish text by Zab Translation.
Other titles: Avicena, el canon de la medicina. English
Description: First American edition. I Minneapolis : Graphic Universe, an imprint of Lerner Publishing Group, Inc. 2023. I Series: Graphic science biographies I "Avicena, el canon de la medicina by Colección Científicos"–Title page verso. I Includes bibliographical references and index. I Audience: Ages 10–14 I Audience: Grades 4–6 I Summary: "Avicenna was a physician and philosopher in an era known as the Islamic Golden Age. His early medical encyclopedia, The Canon of Medicine, was a groundbreaking text that scholars and healers read for centuries afterward"– Provided by publisher.
Identifiers: LCCN 2022039717 (print) I LCCN 2022039718 (ebook) I ISBN 9781728442938 (lib bdg) I ISBN 9781728478289 (pbk) I ISBN 9781728480619 (eb pdf)
Subjects: LCSH: Avicenna, 980–1037–Juvenile literature. I Muslim philosophers–Biography–Juvenile literature. I Muslim philosophers–Biography–Comic books, strips, etc. I Scientists–Asia, Central–Biography–Juvenile literature. I Medicine, Persian–History–Juvenile literature. I BISAC: JUVENILE NONFICTION / Comics & Graphic Novels / Biography & Memoir I JUVENILE NONFICTION / Biography & Autobiography / Literary
Classification: LCC B751.Z7 B39 2023 (print) I LCC B751.Z7 (ebook) I DDC 181/.5–dc23/eng/20221020

LC record available at https://lccn.loc.gov/2022039717
LC ebook record available at https://lccn.loc.gov/2022039718

Manufactured in the United States of America
3-1009735-49808-5/31/2023

CONTENTS

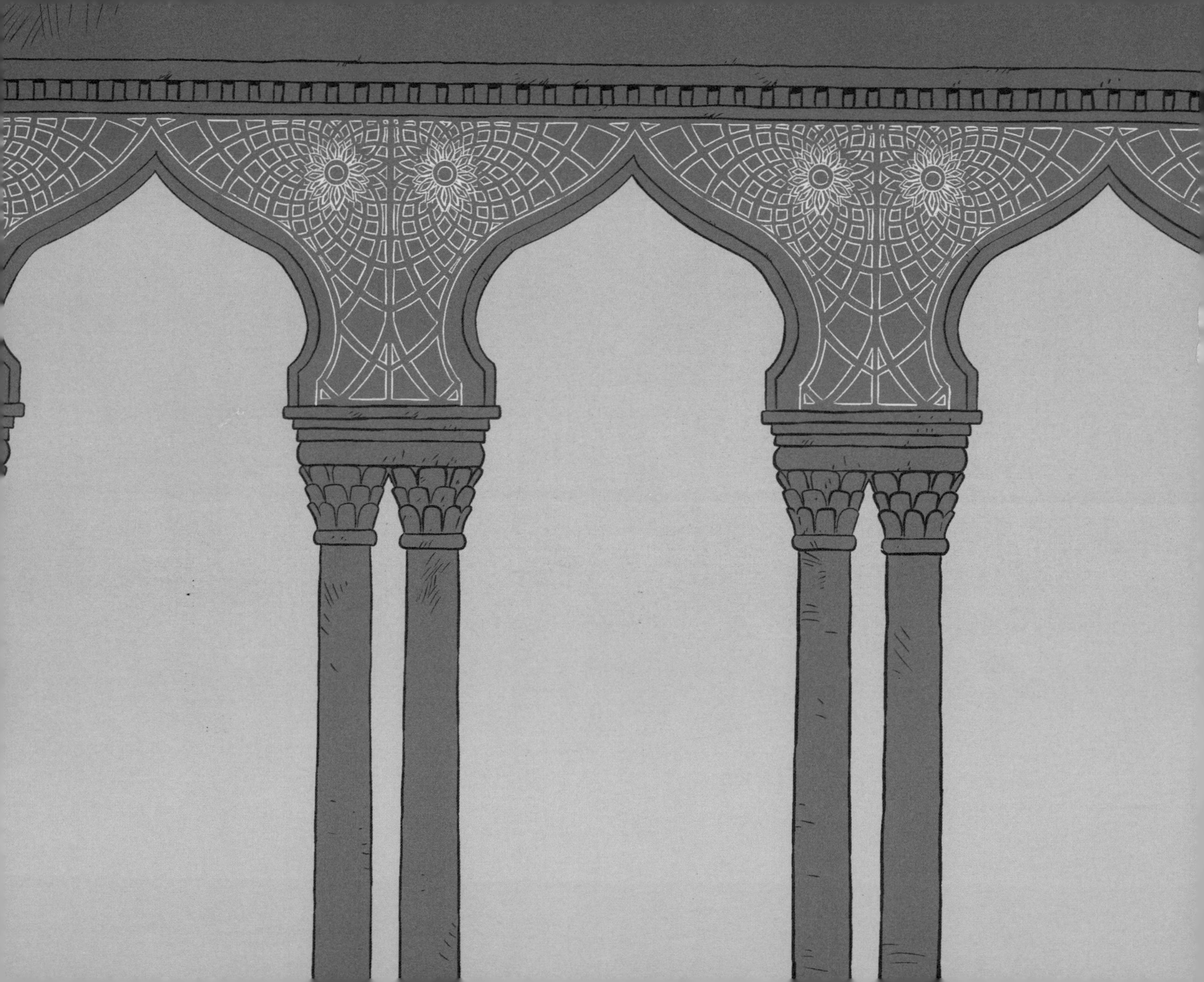

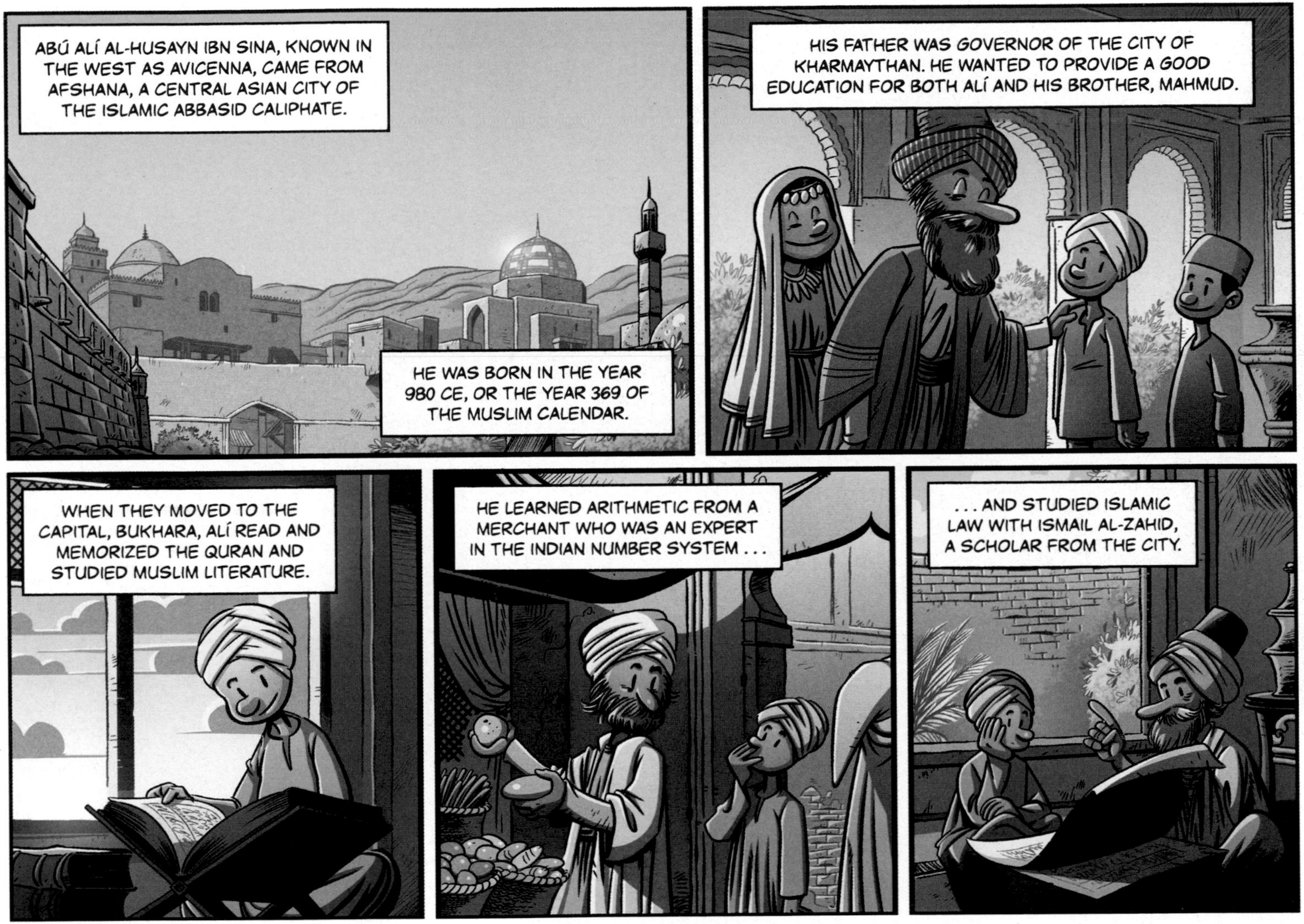
ABÚ ALÍ AL-HUSAYN IBN SINA, KNOWN IN THE WEST AS AVICENNA, CAME FROM AFSHANA, A CENTRAL ASIAN CITY OF THE ISLAMIC ABBASID CALIPHATE.
HE WAS BORN IN THE YEAR 980 CE, OR THE YEAR 369 OF THE MUSLIM CALENDAR.
HIS FATHER WAS GOVERNOR OF THE CITY OF KHARMAYTHAN. HE WANTED TO PROVIDE A GOOD EDUCATION FOR BOTH ALÍ AND HIS BROTHER, MAHMUD.
WHEN THEY MOVED TO THE CAPITAL, BUKHARA, ALÍ READ AND MEMORIZED THE QURAN AND STUDIED MUSLIM LITERATURE.
HE LEARNED ARITHMETIC FROM A MERCHANT WHO WAS AN EXPERT IN THE INDIAN NUMBER SYSTEM . . .
. . . AND STUDIED ISLAMIC LAW WITH ISMAIL AL-ZAHID, A SCHOLAR FROM THE CITY.

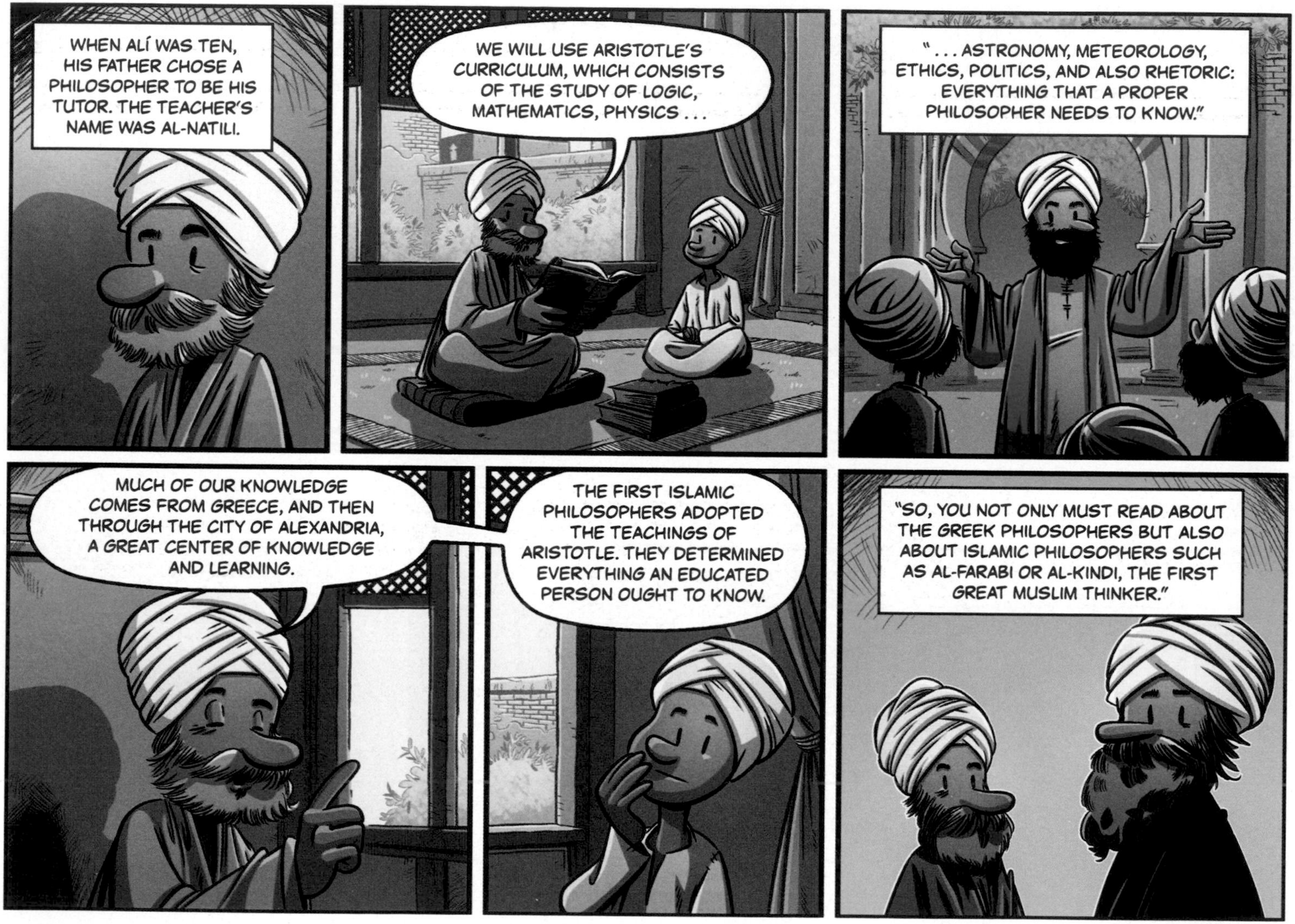
WHEN ALÍ WAS TEN, HIS FATHER CHOSE A PHILOSOPHER TO BE HIS TUTOR. THE TEACHER'S NAME WAS AL-NATILI.
WE WILL USE ARISTOTLE'S CURRICULUM, WHICH CONSISTS OF THE STUDY OF LOGIC, MATHEMATICS, PHYSICS . . .
" . . . ASTRONOMY, METEOROLOGY, ETHICS, POLITICS, AND ALSO RHETORIC: EVERYTHING THAT A PROPER PHILOSOPHER NEEDS TO KNOW."
MUCH OF OUR KNOWLEDGE COMES FROM GREECE, AND THEN THROUGH THE CITY OF ALEXANDRIA, A GREAT CENTER OF KNOWLEDGE AND LEARNING.
THE FIRST ISLAMIC PHILOSOPHERS ADOPTED THE TEACHINGS OF ARISTOTLE. THEY DETERMINED EVERYTHING AN EDUCATED PERSON OUGHT TO KNOW.
"SO, YOU NOT ONLY MUST READ ABOUT THE GREEK PHILOSOPHERS BUT ALSO ABOUT ISLAMIC PHILOSOPHERS SUCH AS AL-FARABI OR AL-KINDI, THE FIRST GREAT MUSLIM THINKER."

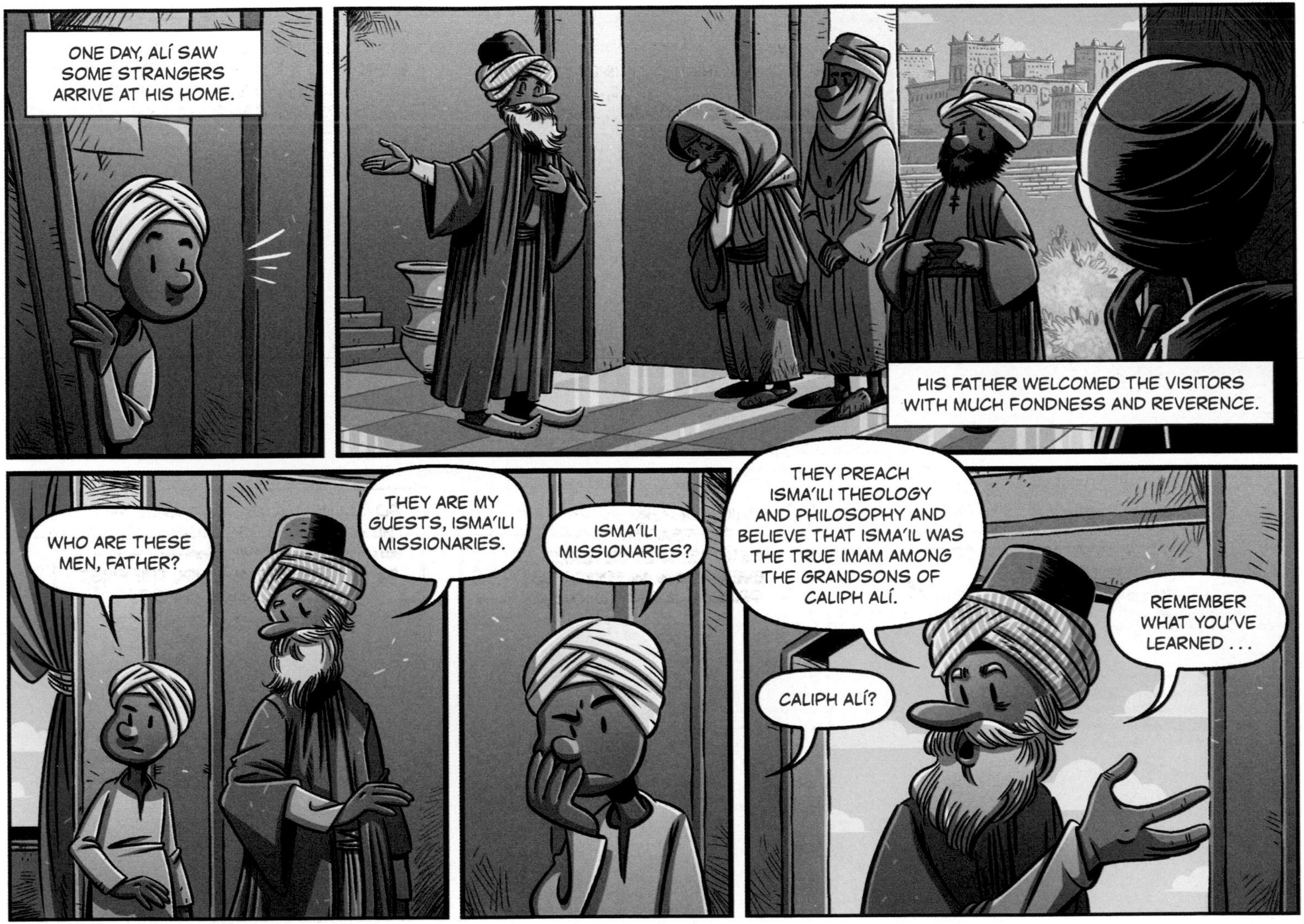
ONE DAY, ALÍ SAW SOME STRANGERS ARRIVE AT HIS HOME.
HIS FATHER WELCOMED THE VISITORS WITH MUCH FONDNESS AND REVERENCE.
WHO ARE THESE MEN, FATHER?
THEY ARE MY GUESTS, ISMA'ILI MISSIONARIES.
ISMA'ILI MISSIONARIES?
THEY PREACH ISMA'ILI THEOLOGY AND PHILOSOPHY AND BELIEVE THAT ISMA'IL WAS THE TRUE IMAM AMONG THE GRANDSONS OF CALIPH ALÍ.
CALIPH ALÍ?
REMEMBER WHAT YOU'VE LEARNED . . .

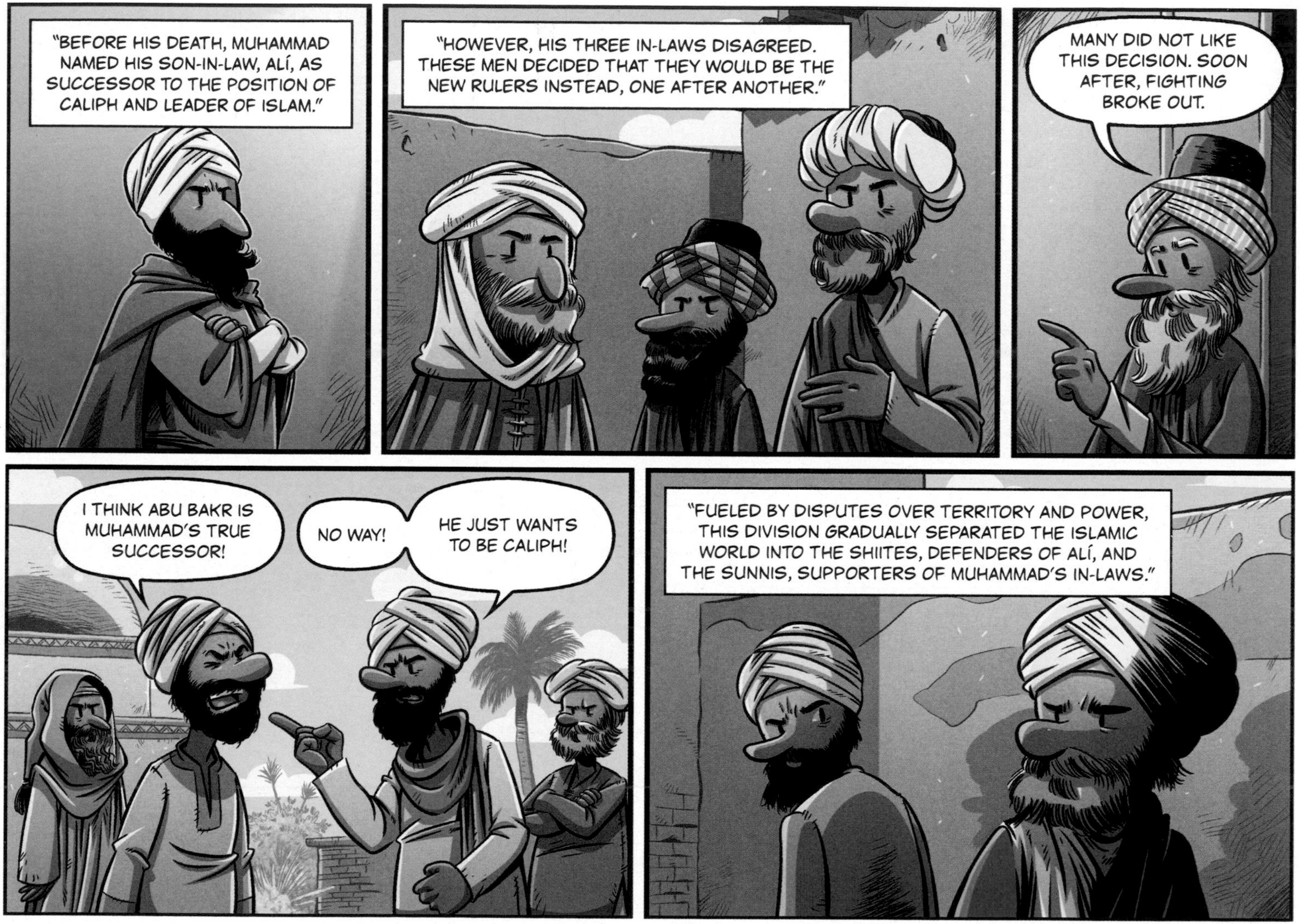
"BEFORE HIS DEATH, MUHAMMAD NAMED HIS SON-IN-LAW, ALÍ, AS SUCCESSOR TO THE POSITION OF CALIPH AND LEADER OF ISLAM."
"HOWEVER, HIS THREE IN-LAWS DISAGREED. THESE MEN DECIDED THAT THEY WOULD BE THE NEW RULERS INSTEAD, ONE AFTER ANOTHER."
MANY DID NOT LIKE THIS DECISION. SOON AFTER, FIGHTING BROKE OUT.
I THINK ABU BAKR IS MUHAMMAD'S TRUE SUCCESSOR!
NO WAY!
HE JUST WANTS TO BE CALIPH!
"FUELED BY DISPUTES OVER TERRITORY AND POWER, THIS DIVISION GRADUALLY SEPARATED THE ISLAMIC WORLD INTO THE SHIITES, DEFENDERS OF ALÍ, AND THE SUNNIS, SUPPORTERS OF MUHAMMAD'S IN-LAWS."

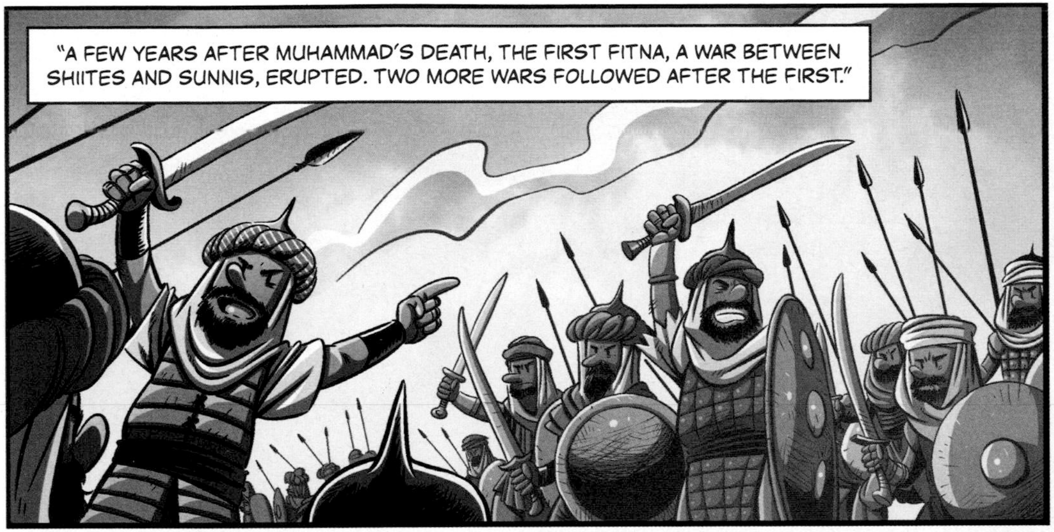
"A FEW YEARS AFTER MUHAMMAD'S DEATH, THE FIRST FITNA, A WAR BETWEEN SHIITES AND SUNNIS, ERUPTED. TWO MORE WARS FOLLOWED AFTER THE FIRST."

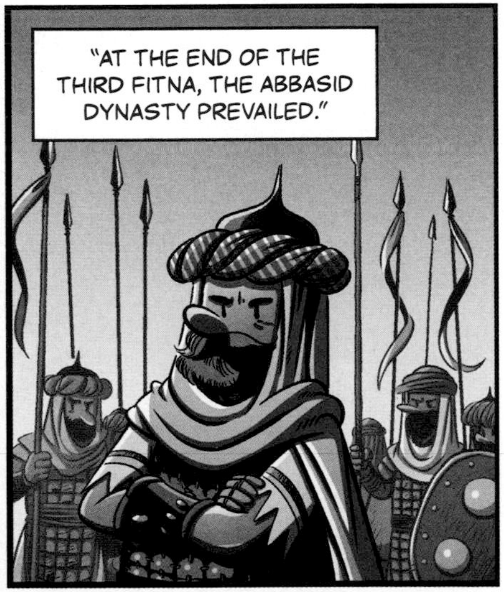
"AT THE END OF THE THIRD FITNA, THE ABBASID DYNASTY PREVAILED."

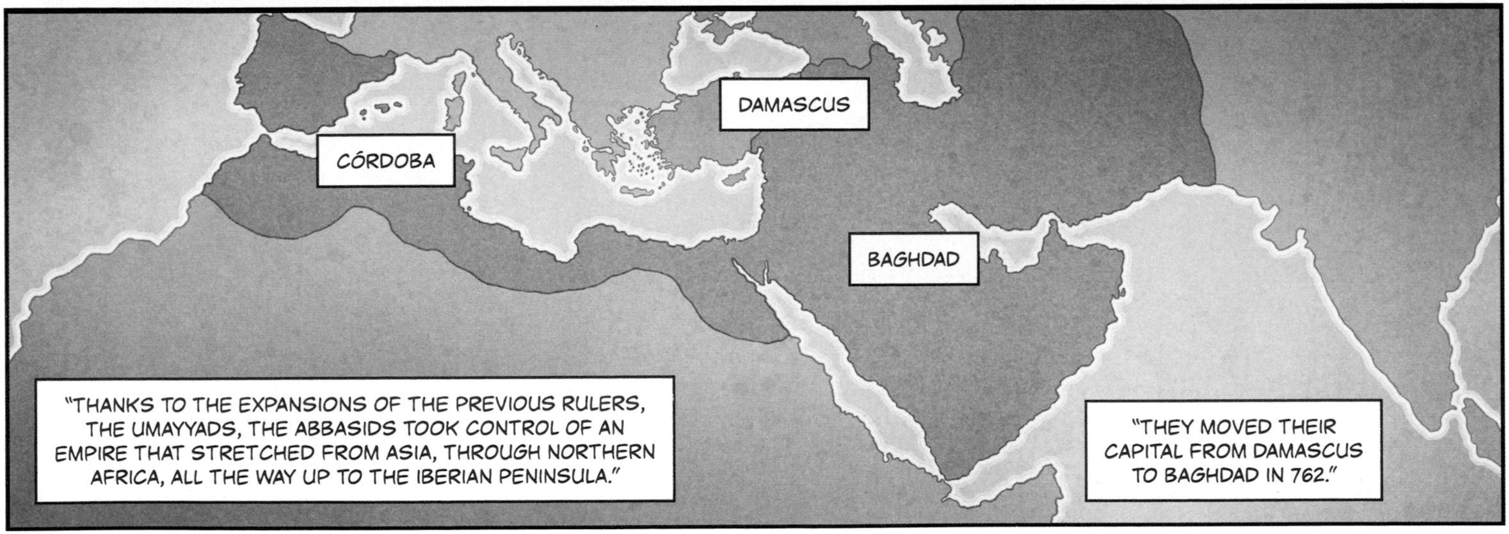
DAMASCUS
CÓRDOBA
BAGHDAD
"THANKS TO THE EXPANSIONS OF THE PREVIOUS RULERS, THE UMAYYADS, THE ABBASIDS TOOK CONTROL OF AN EMPIRE THAT STRETCHED FROM ASIA, THROUGH NORTHERN AFRICA, ALL THE WAY UP TO THE IBERIAN PENINSULA."
"THEY MOVED THEIR CAPITAL FROM DAMASCUS TO BAGHDAD IN 762."

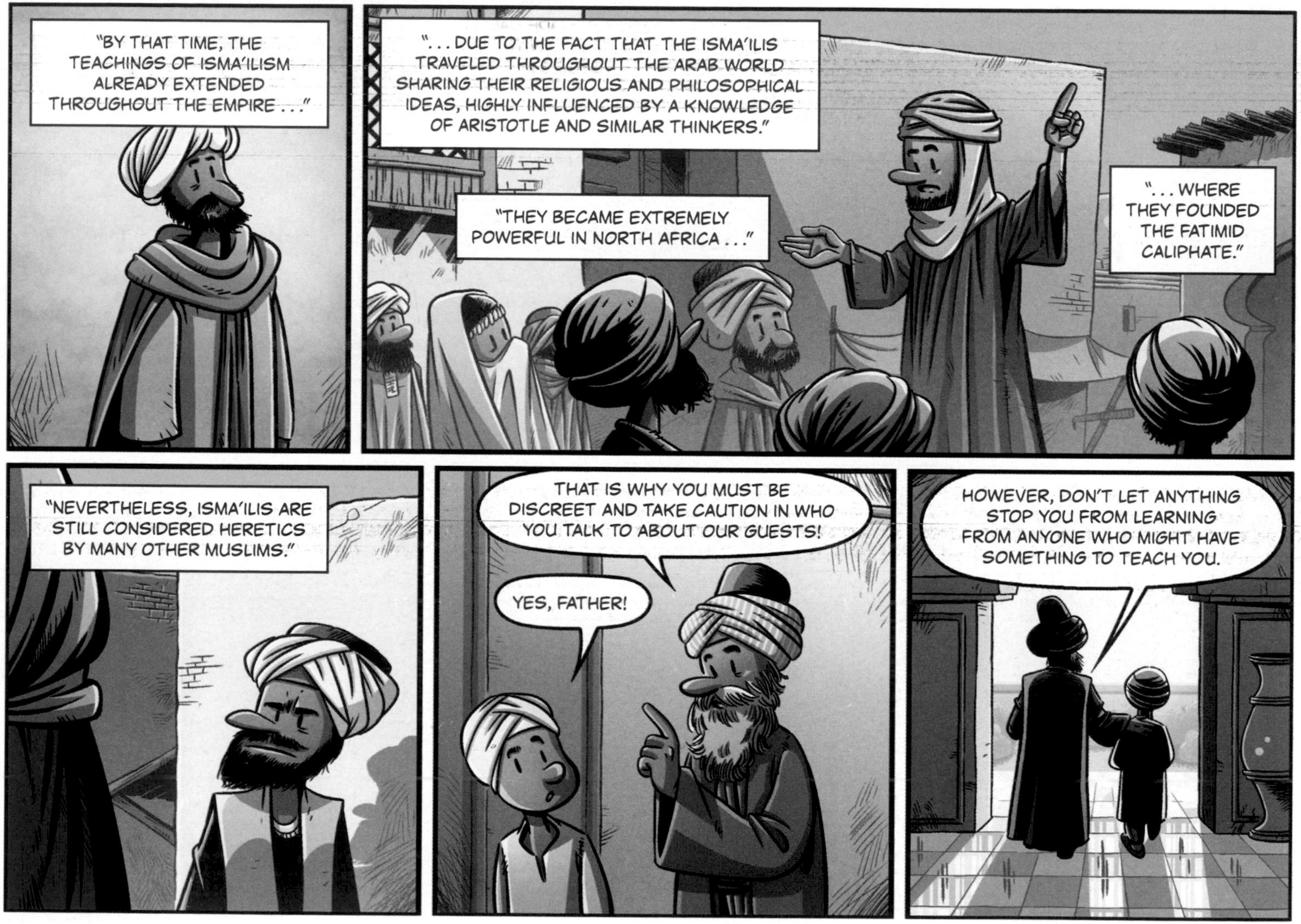
"BY THAT TIME, THE TEACHINGS OF ISMA'ILISM ALREADY EXTENDED THROUGHOUT THE EMPIRE . . ."
". . . DUE TO THE FACT THAT THE ISMA'ILIS TRAVELED THROUGHOUT THE ARAB WORLD SHARING THEIR RELIGIOUS AND PHILOSOPHICAL IDEAS, HIGHLY INFLUENCED BY A KNOWLEDGE OF ARISTOTLE AND SIMILAR THINKERS."
"THEY BECAME EXTREMELY POWERFUL IN NORTH AFRICA . . ."
". . . WHERE THEY FOUNDED THE FATIMID CALIPHATE."
"NEVERTHELESS, ISMA'ILIS ARE STILL CONSIDERED HERETICS BY MANY OTHER MUSLIMS."
THAT IS WHY YOU MUST BE DISCREET AND TAKE CAUTION IN WHO YOU TALK TO ABOUT OUR GUESTS!
YES, FATHER!
HOWEVER, DON'T LET ANYTHING STOP YOU FROM LEARNING FROM ANYONE WHO MIGHT HAVE SOMETHING TO TEACH YOU.

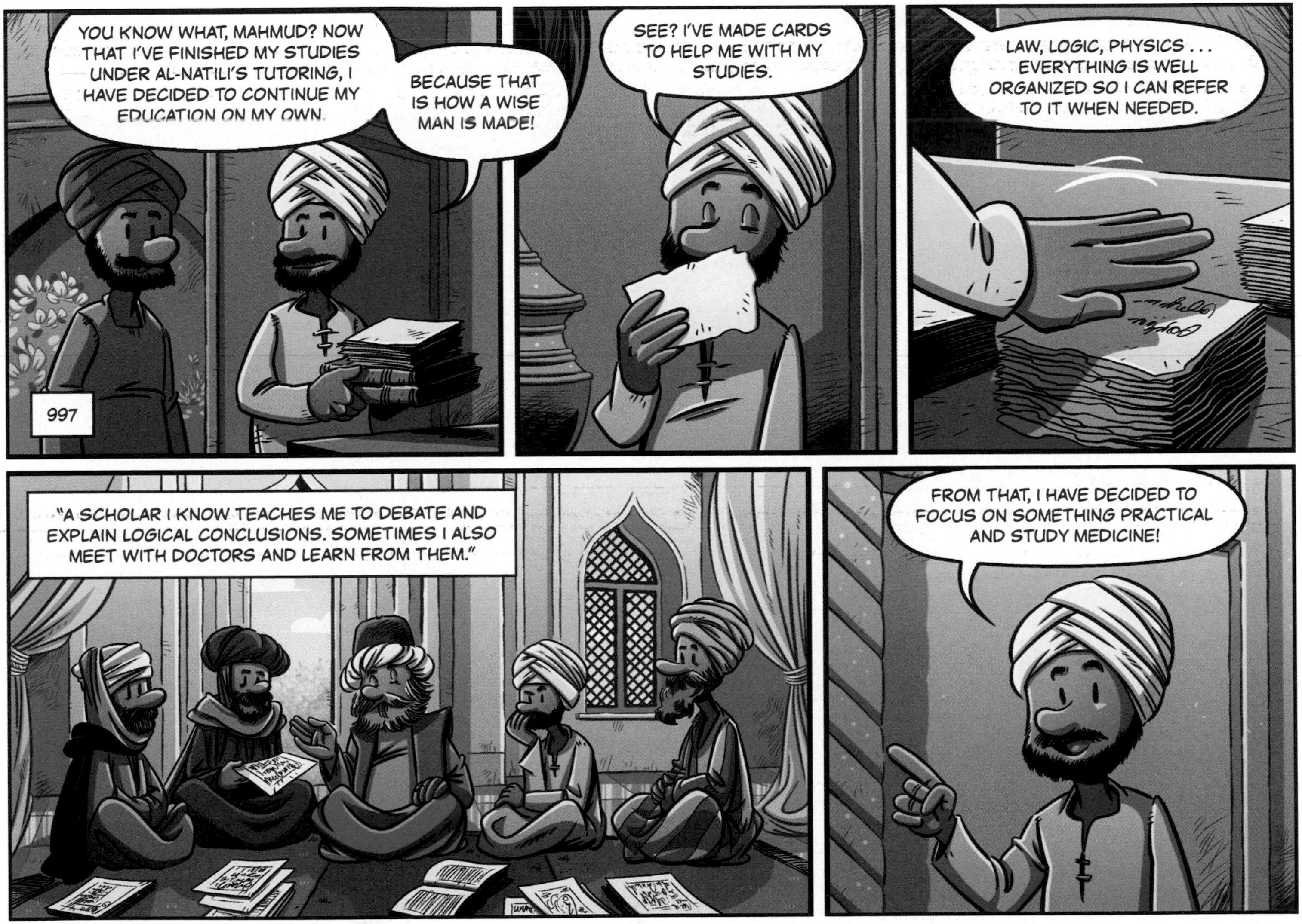
YOU KNOW WHAT, MAHMUD? NOW THAT I'VE FINISHED MY STUDIES UNDER AL-NATILI'S TUTORING, I HAVE DECIDED TO CONTINUE MY EDUCATION ON MY OWN.
BECAUSE THAT IS HOW A WISE MAN IS MADE!
997
SEE? I'VE MADE CARDS TO HELP ME WITH MY STUDIES.
LAW, LOGIC, PHYSICS . . . EVERYTHING IS WELL ORGANIZED SO I CAN REFER TO IT WHEN NEEDED.
"A SCHOLAR I KNOW TEACHES ME TO DEBATE AND EXPLAIN LOGICAL CONCLUSIONS. SOMETIMES I ALSO MEET WITH DOCTORS AND LEARN FROM THEM."
FROM THAT, I HAVE DECIDED TO FOCUS ON SOMETHING PRACTICAL AND STUDY MEDICINE!

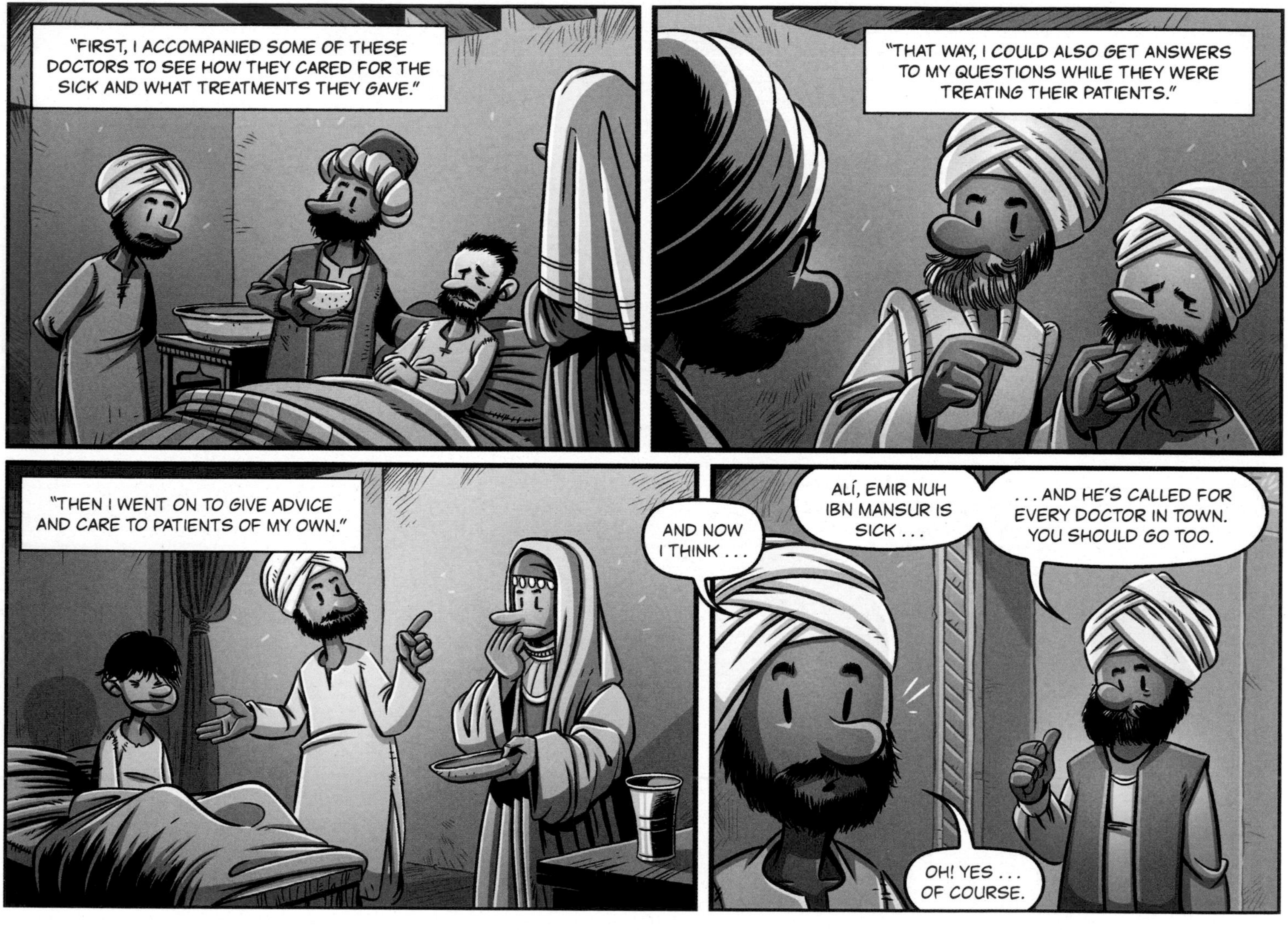
"FIRST, I ACCOMPANIED SOME OF THESE DOCTORS TO SEE HOW THEY CARED FOR THE SICK AND WHAT TREATMENTS THEY GAVE."
"THAT WAY, I COULD ALSO GET ANSWERS TO MY QUESTIONS WHILE THEY WERE TREATING THEIR PATIENTS."
"THEN I WENT ON TO GIVE ADVICE AND CARE TO PATIENTS OF MY OWN."
AND NOW I THINK . . .
ALÍ, EMIR NUH IBN MANSUR IS SICK . . .
. . . AND HE'S CALLED FOR EVERY DOCTOR IN TOWN. YOU SHOULD GO TOO.
OH! YES . . . OF COURSE.

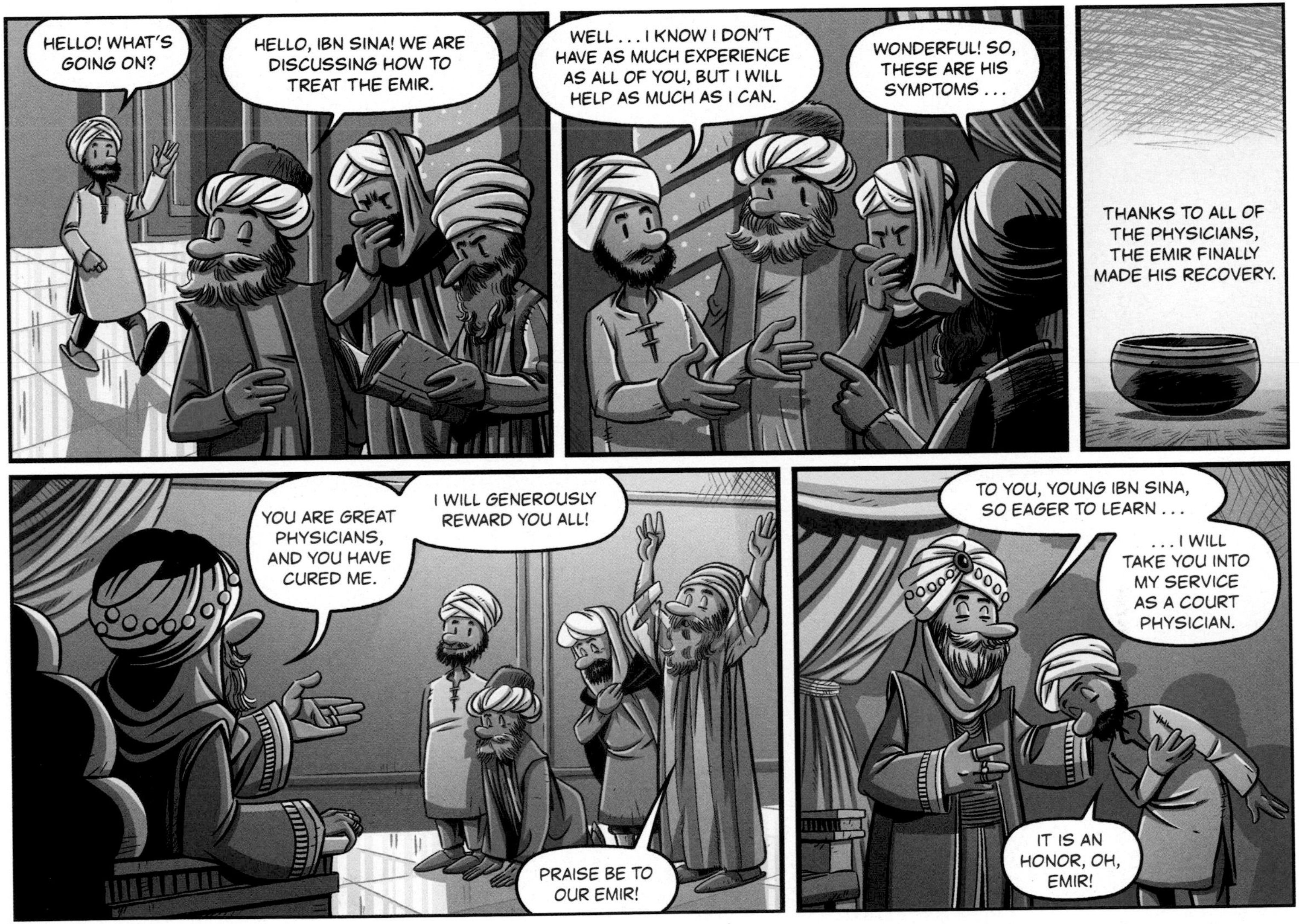
HELLO! WHAT'S GOING ON?
HELLO, IBN SINA! WE ARE DISCUSSING HOW TO TREAT THE EMIR.
WELL . . . I KNOW I DON'T HAVE AS MUCH EXPERIENCE AS ALL OF YOU, BUT I WILL HELP AS MUCH AS I CAN.
WONDERFUL! SO, THESE ARE HIS SYMPTOMS . . .
THANKS TO ALL OF THE PHYSICIANS, THE EMIR FINALLY MADE HIS RECOVERY.
YOU ARE GREAT PHYSICIANS, AND YOU HAVE CURED ME.
I WILL GENEROUSLY REWARD YOU ALL!
PRAISE BE TO OUR EMIR!
TO YOU, YOUNG IBN SINA, SO EAGER TO LEARN . . .
. . . I WILL TAKE YOU INTO MY SERVICE AS A COURT PHYSICIAN.
IT IS AN HONOR, OH, EMIR!

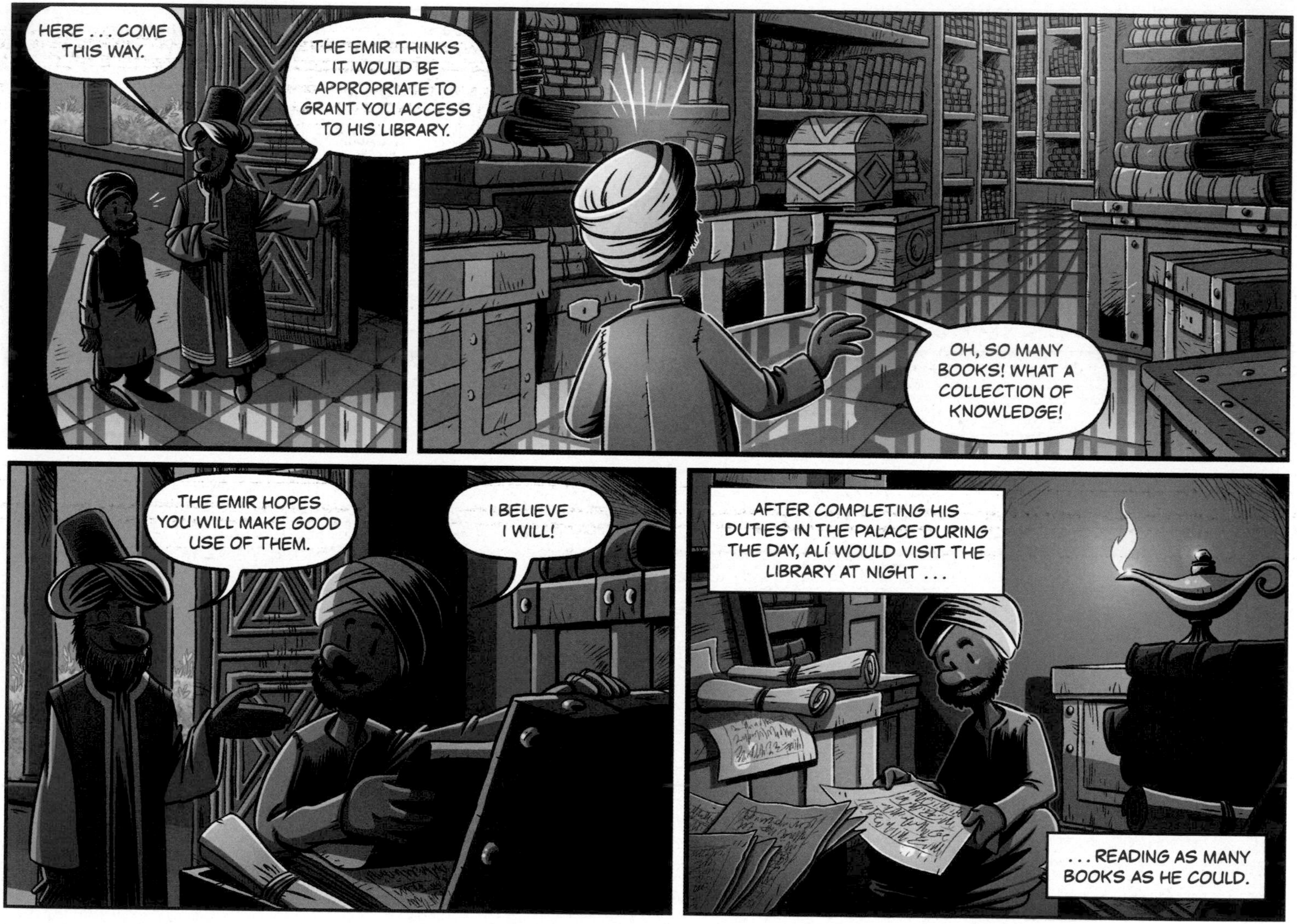
HERE . . . COME THIS WAY.
THE EMIR THINKS IT WOULD BE APPROPRIATE TO GRANT YOU ACCESS TO HIS LIBRARY.
OH, SO MANY BOOKS! WHAT A COLLECTION OF KNOWLEDGE!
THE EMIR HOPES YOU WILL MAKE GOOD USE OF THEM.
I BELIEVE I WILL!
AFTER COMPLETING HIS DUTIES IN THE PALACE DURING THE DAY, ALÍ WOULD VISIT THE LIBRARY AT NIGHT . . .
. . . READING AS MANY BOOKS AS HE COULD.

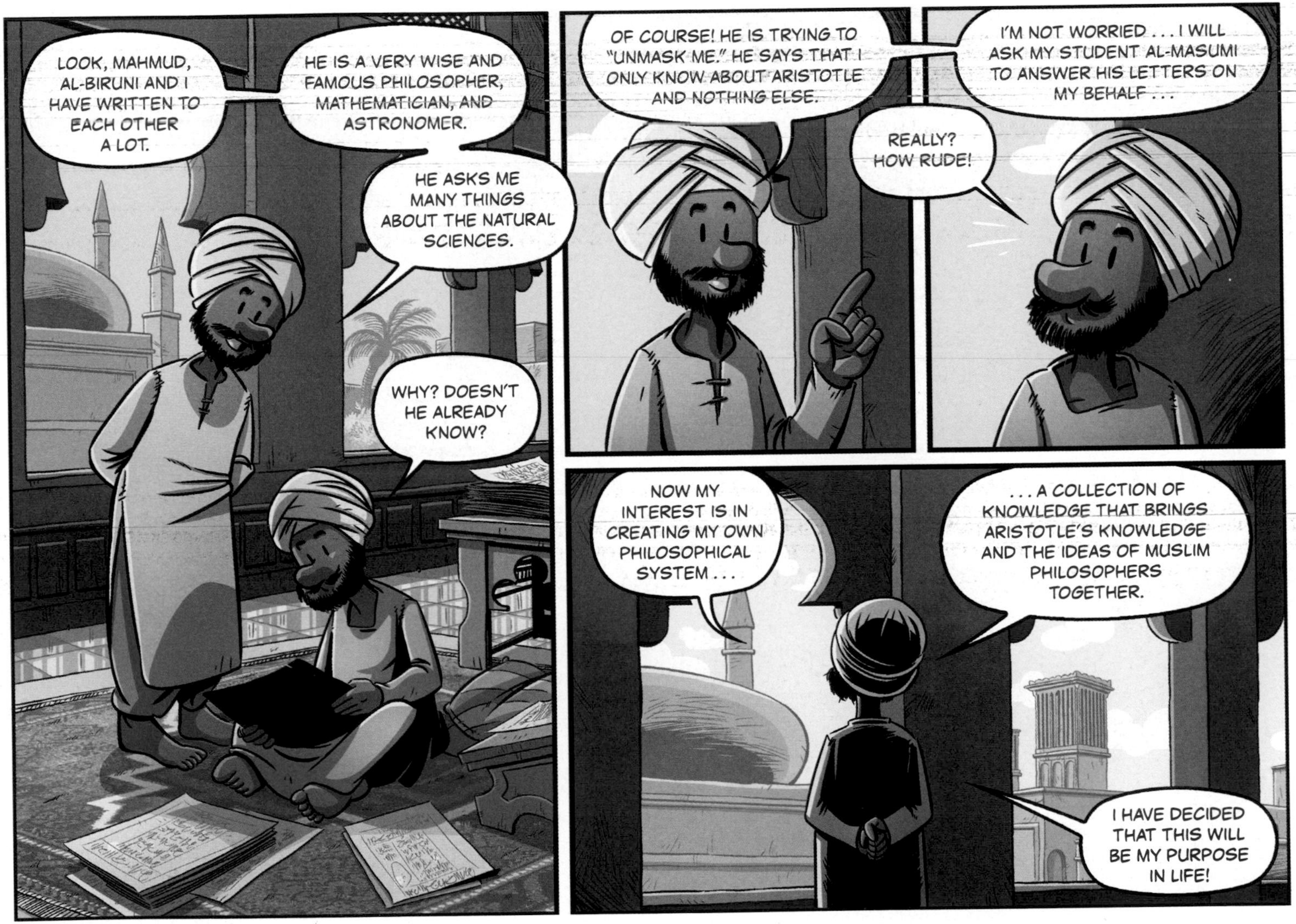
LOOK, MAHMUD, AL-BIRUNI AND I HAVE WRITTEN TO EACH OTHER A LOT.
HE IS A VERY WISE AND FAMOUS PHILOSOPHER, MATHEMATICIAN, AND ASTRONOMER.
HE ASKS ME MANY THINGS ABOUT THE NATURAL SCIENCES.
WHY? DOESN'T HE ALREADY KNOW?
OF COURSE! HE IS TRYING TO "UNMASK ME." HE SAYS THAT I ONLY KNOW ABOUT ARISTOTLE AND NOTHING ELSE.
REALLY? HOW RUDE!
I'M NOT WORRIED . . . I WILL ASK MY STUDENT AL-MASUMI TO ANSWER HIS LETTERS ON MY BEHALF . . .
NOW MY INTEREST IS IN CREATING MY OWN PHILOSOPHICAL SYSTEM . . .
. . . A COLLECTION OF KNOWLEDGE THAT BRINGS ARISTOTLE'S KNOWLEDGE AND THE IDEAS OF MUSLIM PHILOSOPHERS TOGETHER.
I HAVE DECIDED THAT THIS WILL BE MY PURPOSE IN LIFE!

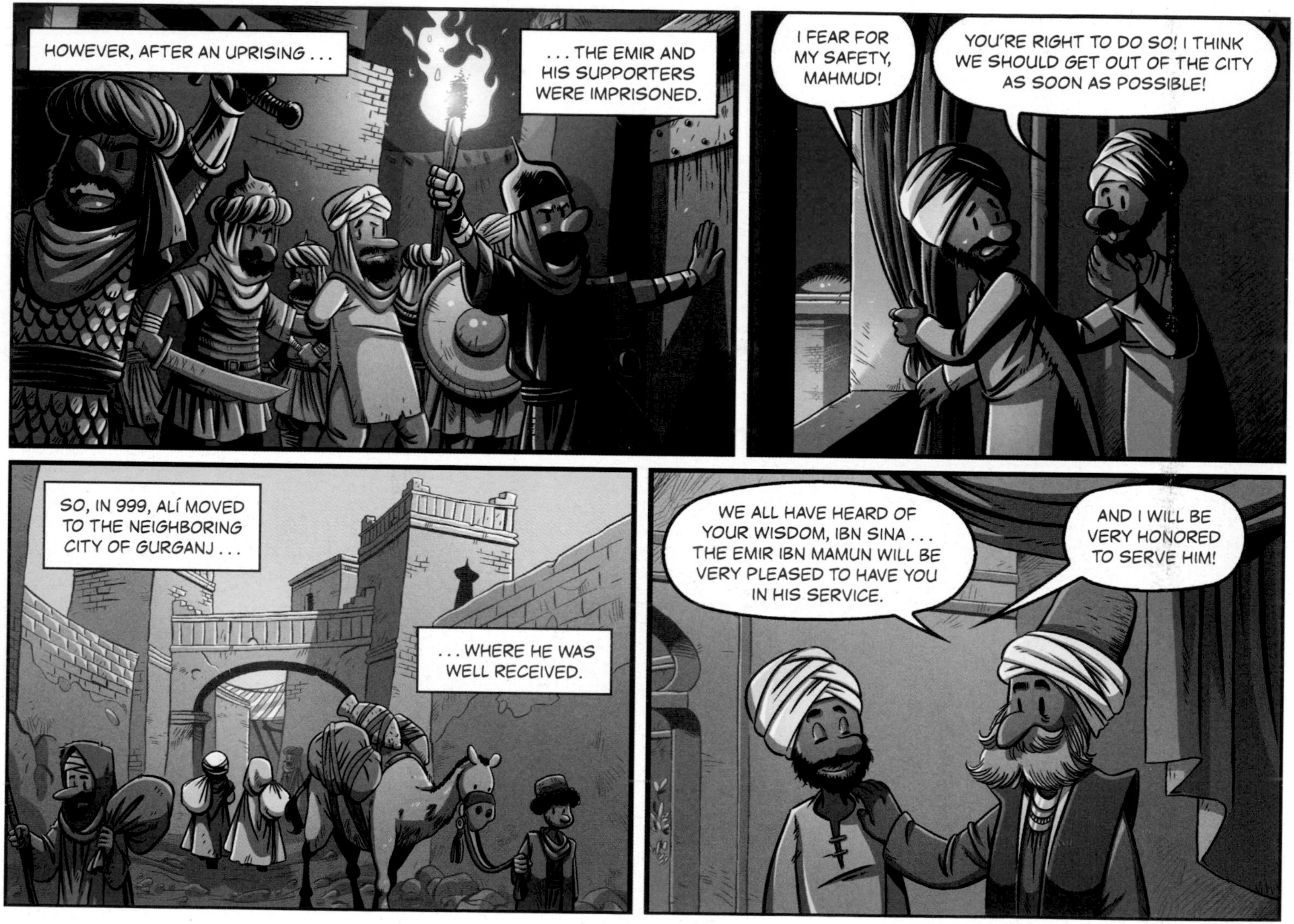

HOWEVER, AFTER AN UPRISING . . .
. . . THE EMIR AND HIS SUPPORTERS WERE IMPRISONED.
I FEAR FOR MY SAFETY, MAHMUD!
YOU'RE RIGHT TO DO SO! I THINK WE SHOULD GET OUT OF THE CITY AS SOON AS POSSIBLE!
SO, IN 999, ALÍ MOVED TO THE NEIGHBORING CITY OF GURGANJ . . .
. . . WHERE HE WAS WELL RECEIVED.
WE ALL HAVE HEARD OF YOUR WISDOM, IBN SINA . . . THE EMIR IBN MAMUN WILL BE VERY PLEASED TO HAVE YOU IN HIS SERVICE.
AND I WILL BE VERY HONORED TO SERVE HIM!

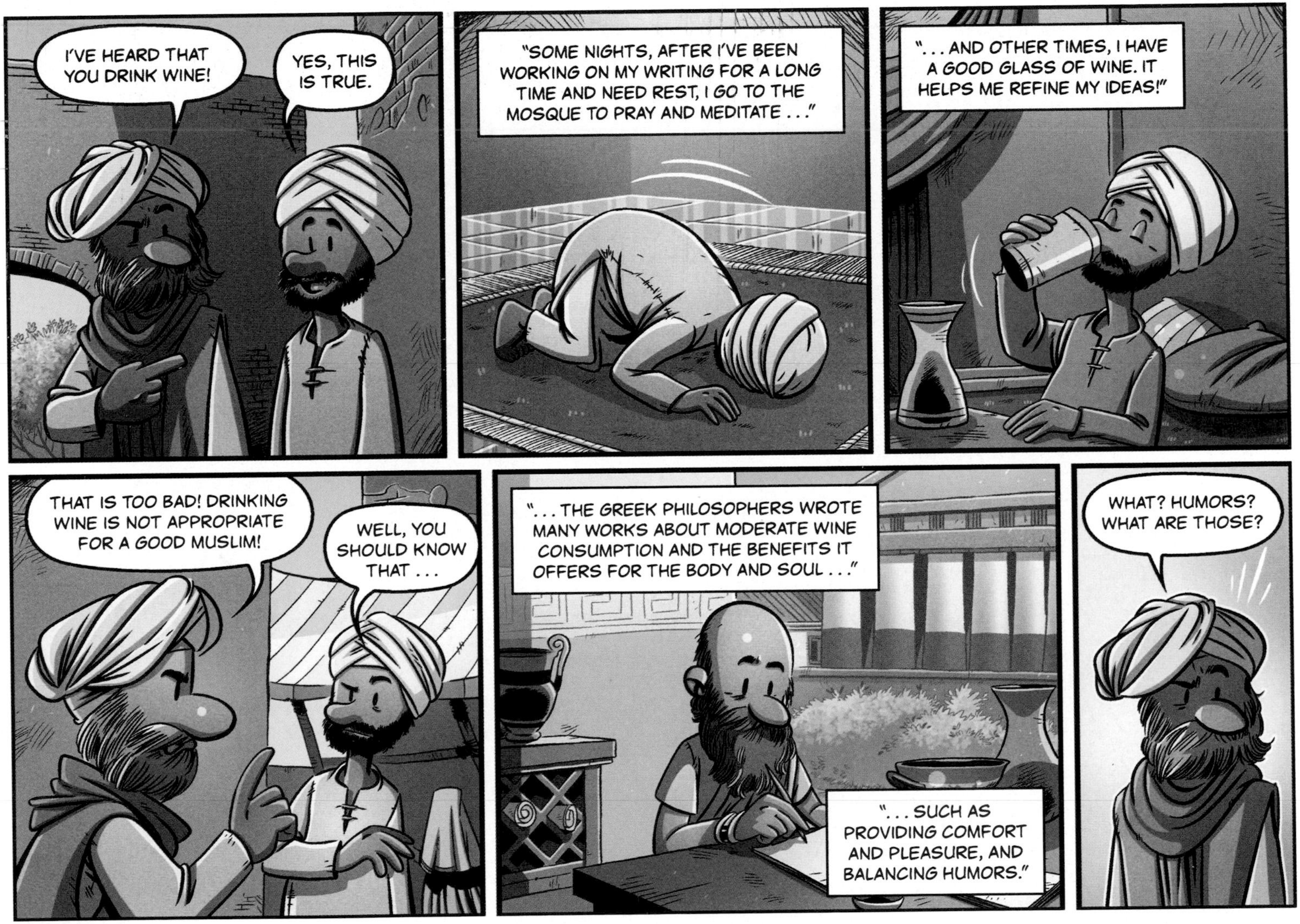
I'VE HEARD THAT YOU DRINK WINE!
YES, THIS IS TRUE.
"SOME NIGHTS, AFTER I'VE BEEN WORKING ON MY WRITING FOR A LONG TIME AND NEED REST, I GO TO THE MOSQUE TO PRAY AND MEDITATE . . ."
". . . AND OTHER TIMES, I HAVE A GOOD GLASS OF WINE. IT HELPS ME REFINE MY IDEAS!"
THAT IS TOO BAD! DRINKING WINE IS NOT APPROPRIATE FOR A GOOD MUSLIM!
WELL, YOU SHOULD KNOW THAT . . .
". . . THE GREEK PHILOSOPHERS WROTE MANY WORKS ABOUT MODERATE WINE CONSUMPTION AND THE BENEFITS IT OFFERS FOR THE BODY AND SOUL . . ."
". . . SUCH AS PROVIDING COMFORT AND PLEASURE, AND BALANCING HUMORS."
WHAT? HUMORS? WHAT ARE THOSE?

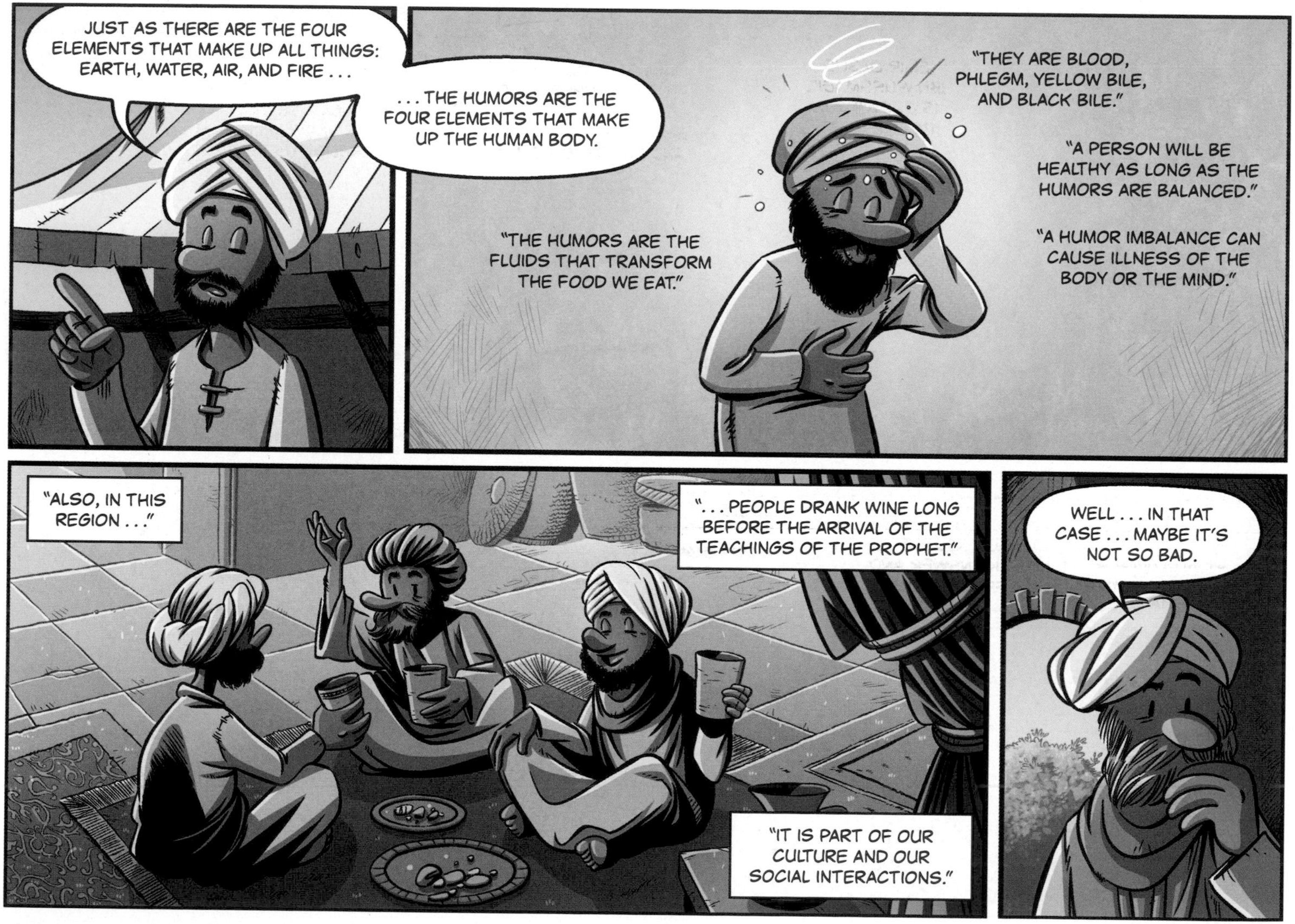
JUST AS THERE ARE THE FOUR ELEMENTS THAT MAKE UP ALL THINGS: EARTH, WATER, AIR, AND FIRE . . .
. . . THE HUMORS ARE THE FOUR ELEMENTS THAT MAKE UP THE HUMAN BODY.
"THE HUMORS ARE THE FLUIDS THAT TRANSFORM THE FOOD WE EAT."
"THEY ARE BLOOD, PHLEGM, YELLOW BILE, AND BLACK BILE."
"A PERSON WILL BE HEALTHY AS LONG AS THE HUMORS ARE BALANCED."
"A HUMOR IMBALANCE CAN CAUSE ILLNESS OF THE BODY OR THE MIND."
"ALSO, IN THIS REGION . . ."
". . . PEOPLE DRANK WINE LONG BEFORE THE ARRIVAL OF THE TEACHINGS OF THE PROPHET."
"IT IS PART OF OUR CULTURE AND OUR SOCIAL INTERACTIONS."
WELL . . . IN THAT CASE . . . MAYBE IT'S NOT SO BAD.

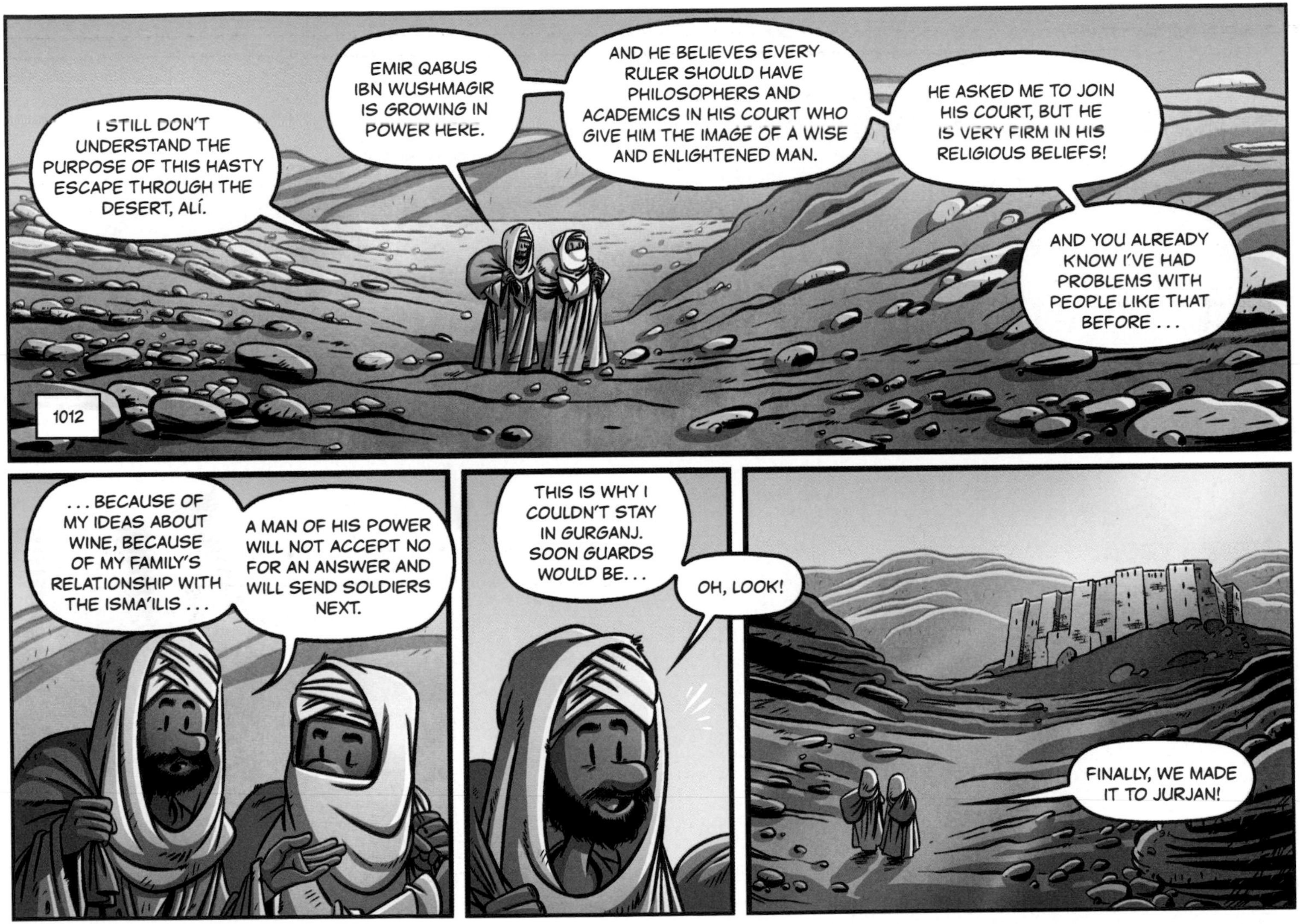
1012
I STILL DON'T UNDERSTAND THE PURPOSE OF THIS HASTY ESCAPE THROUGH THE DESERT, ALÍ.
EMIR QABUS IBN WUSHMAGIR IS GROWING IN POWER HERE.
AND HE BELIEVES EVERY RULER SHOULD HAVE PHILOSOPHERS AND ACADEMICS IN HIS COURT WHO GIVE HIM THE IMAGE OF A WISE AND ENLIGHTENED MAN.
HE ASKED ME TO JOIN HIS COURT, BUT HE IS VERY FIRM IN HIS RELIGIOUS BELIEFS!
AND YOU ALREADY KNOW I'VE HAD PROBLEMS WITH PEOPLE LIKE THAT BEFORE . . .
. . . BECAUSE OF MY IDEAS ABOUT WINE, BECAUSE OF MY FAMILY'S RELATIONSHIP WITH THE ISMA'ILIS . . .
A MAN OF HIS POWER WILL NOT ACCEPT NO FOR AN ANSWER AND WILL SEND SOLDIERS NEXT.
THIS IS WHY I COULDN'T STAY IN GURGANJ. SOON GUARDS WOULD BE. . .
OH, LOOK!
FINALLY, WE MADE IT TO JURJAN!

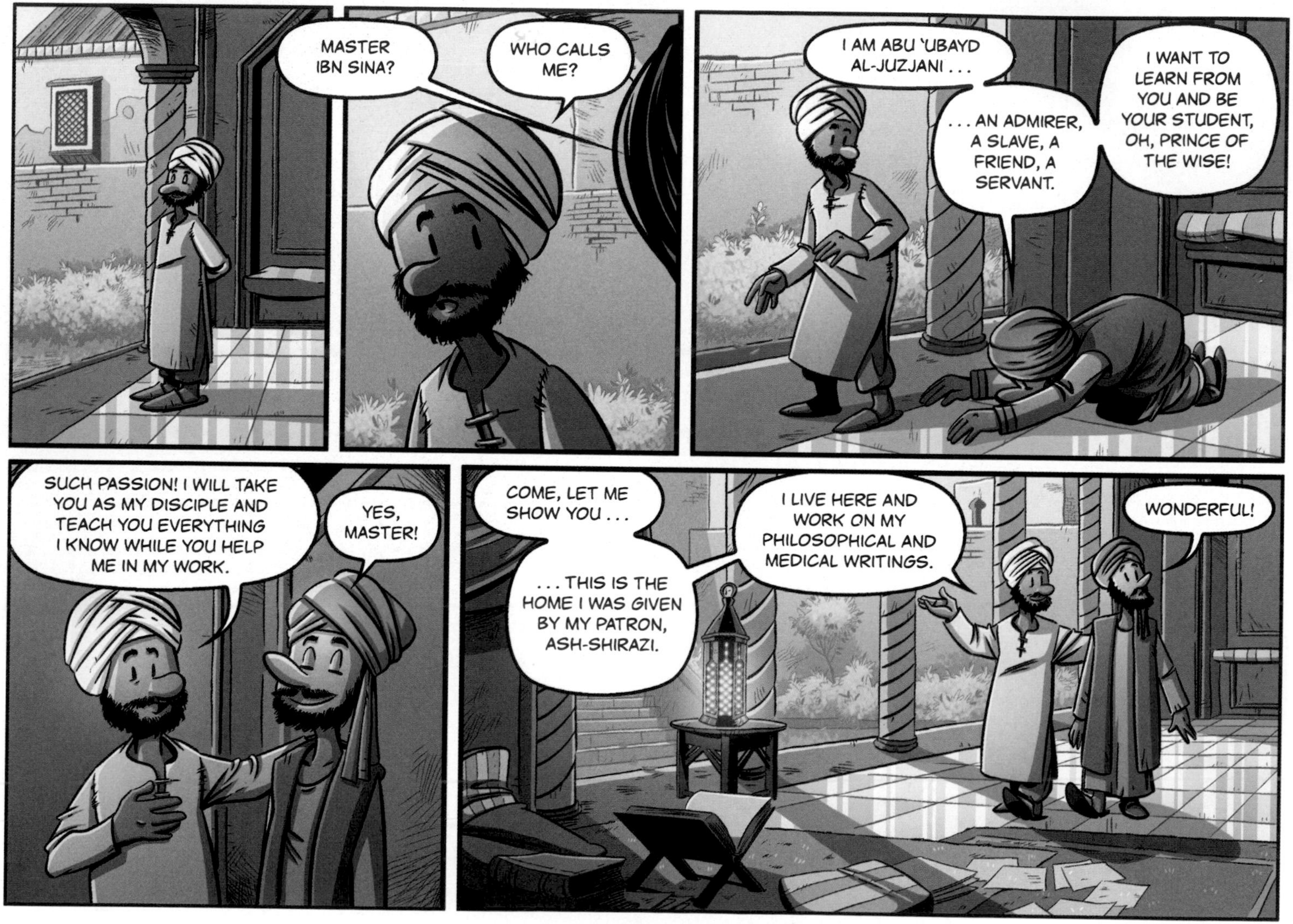
MASTER IBN SINA?
WHO CALLS ME?
I AM ABU 'UBAYD AL-JUZJANI . . .
. . . AN ADMIRER, A SLAVE, A FRIEND, A SERVANT.
I WANT TO LEARN FROM YOU AND BE YOUR STUDENT, OH, PRINCE OF THE WISE!
SUCH PASSION! I WILL TAKE YOU AS MY DISCIPLE AND TEACH YOU EVERYTHING I KNOW WHILE YOU HELP ME IN MY WORK.
YES, MASTER!
COME, LET ME SHOW YOU . . .
. . . THIS IS THE HOME I WAS GIVEN BY MY PATRON, ASH-SHIRAZI.
I LIVE HERE AND WORK ON MY PHILOSOPHICAL AND MEDICAL WRITINGS.
WONDERFUL!

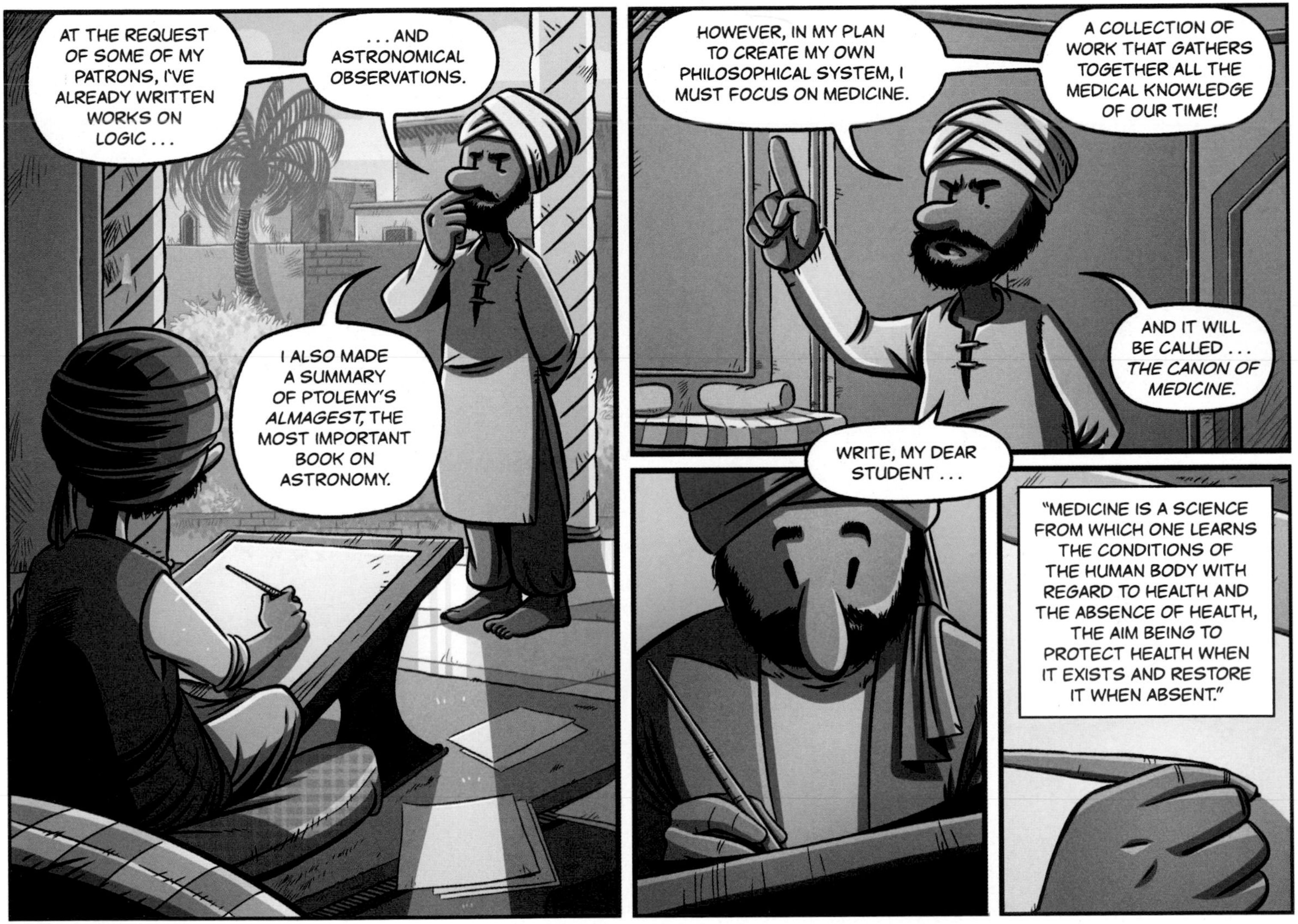
AT THE REQUEST OF SOME OF MY PATRONS, I'VE ALREADY WRITTEN WORKS ON LOGIC . . .
. . . AND ASTRONOMICAL OBSERVATIONS.
I ALSO MADE A SUMMARY OF PTOLEMY'S *ALMAGEST*, THE MOST IMPORTANT BOOK ON ASTRONOMY.
HOWEVER, IN MY PLAN TO CREATE MY OWN PHILOSOPHICAL SYSTEM, I MUST FOCUS ON MEDICINE.
A COLLECTION OF WORK THAT GATHERS TOGETHER ALL THE MEDICAL KNOWLEDGE OF OUR TIME!
AND IT WILL BE CALLED . . . *THE CANON OF MEDICINE.*
WRITE, MY DEAR STUDENT . . .
"MEDICINE IS A SCIENCE FROM WHICH ONE LEARNS THE CONDITIONS OF THE HUMAN BODY WITH REGARD TO HEALTH AND THE ABSENCE OF HEALTH, THE AIM BEING TO PROTECT HEALTH WHEN IT EXISTS AND RESTORE IT WHEN ABSENT."

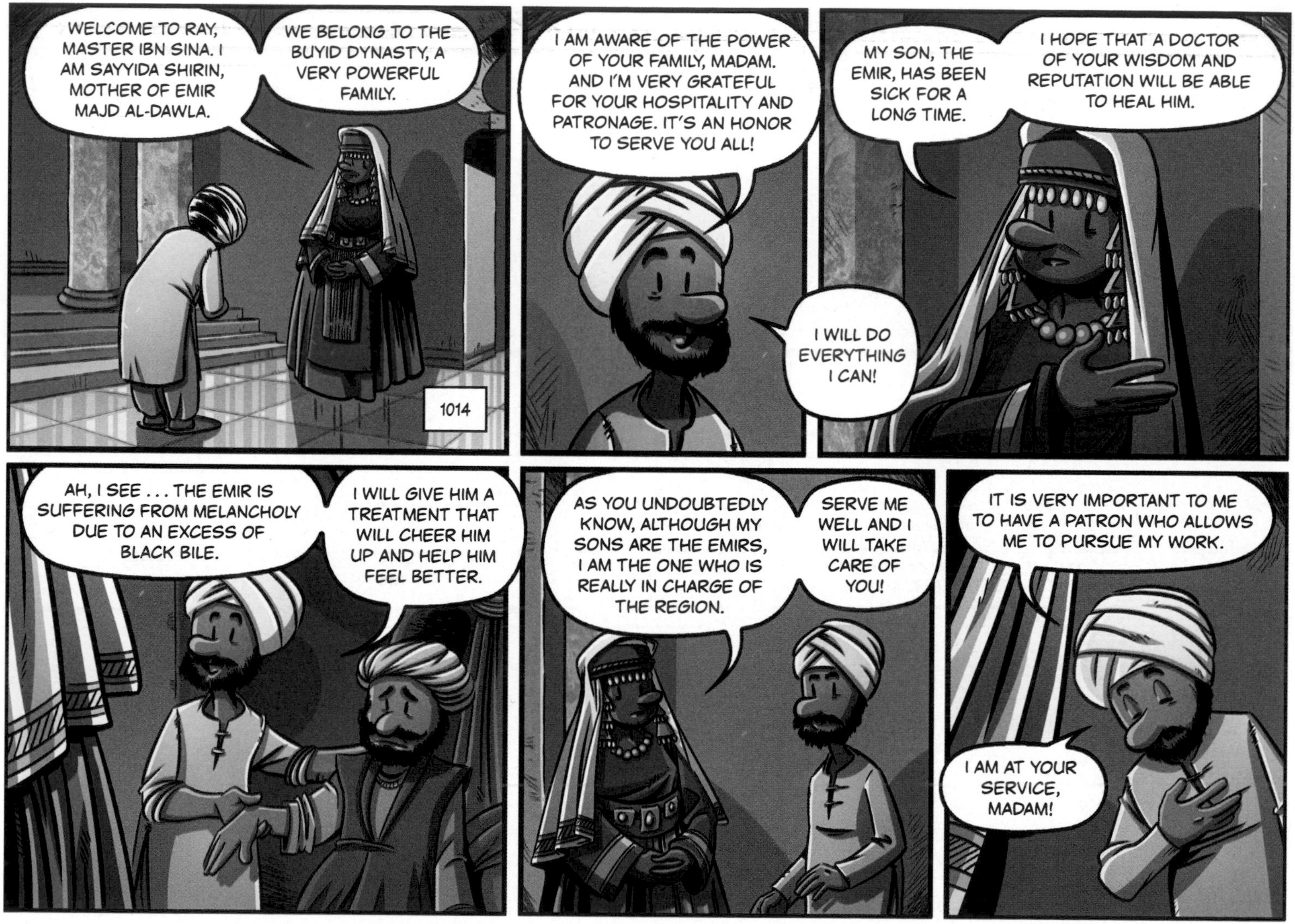
WELCOME TO RAY, MASTER IBN SINA. I AM SAYYIDA SHIRIN, MOTHER OF EMIR MAJD AL-DAWLA.
WE BELONG TO THE BUYID DYNASTY, A VERY POWERFUL FAMILY.
1014
I AM AWARE OF THE POWER OF YOUR FAMILY, MADAM. AND I'M VERY GRATEFUL FOR YOUR HOSPITALITY AND PATRONAGE. IT'S AN HONOR TO SERVE YOU ALL!
MY SON, THE EMIR, HAS BEEN SICK FOR A LONG TIME.
I HOPE THAT A DOCTOR OF YOUR WISDOM AND REPUTATION WILL BE ABLE TO HEAL HIM.
I WILL DO EVERYTHING I CAN!
AH, I SEE . . . THE EMIR IS SUFFERING FROM MELANCHOLY DUE TO AN EXCESS OF BLACK BILE.
I WILL GIVE HIM A TREATMENT THAT WILL CHEER HIM UP AND HELP HIM FEEL BETTER.
AS YOU UNDOUBTEDLY KNOW, ALTHOUGH MY SONS ARE THE EMIRS, I AM THE ONE WHO IS REALLY IN CHARGE OF THE REGION.
SERVE ME WELL AND I WILL TAKE CARE OF YOU!
IT IS VERY IMPORTANT TO ME TO HAVE A PATRON WHO ALLOWS ME TO PURSUE MY WORK.
I AM AT YOUR SERVICE, MADAM!

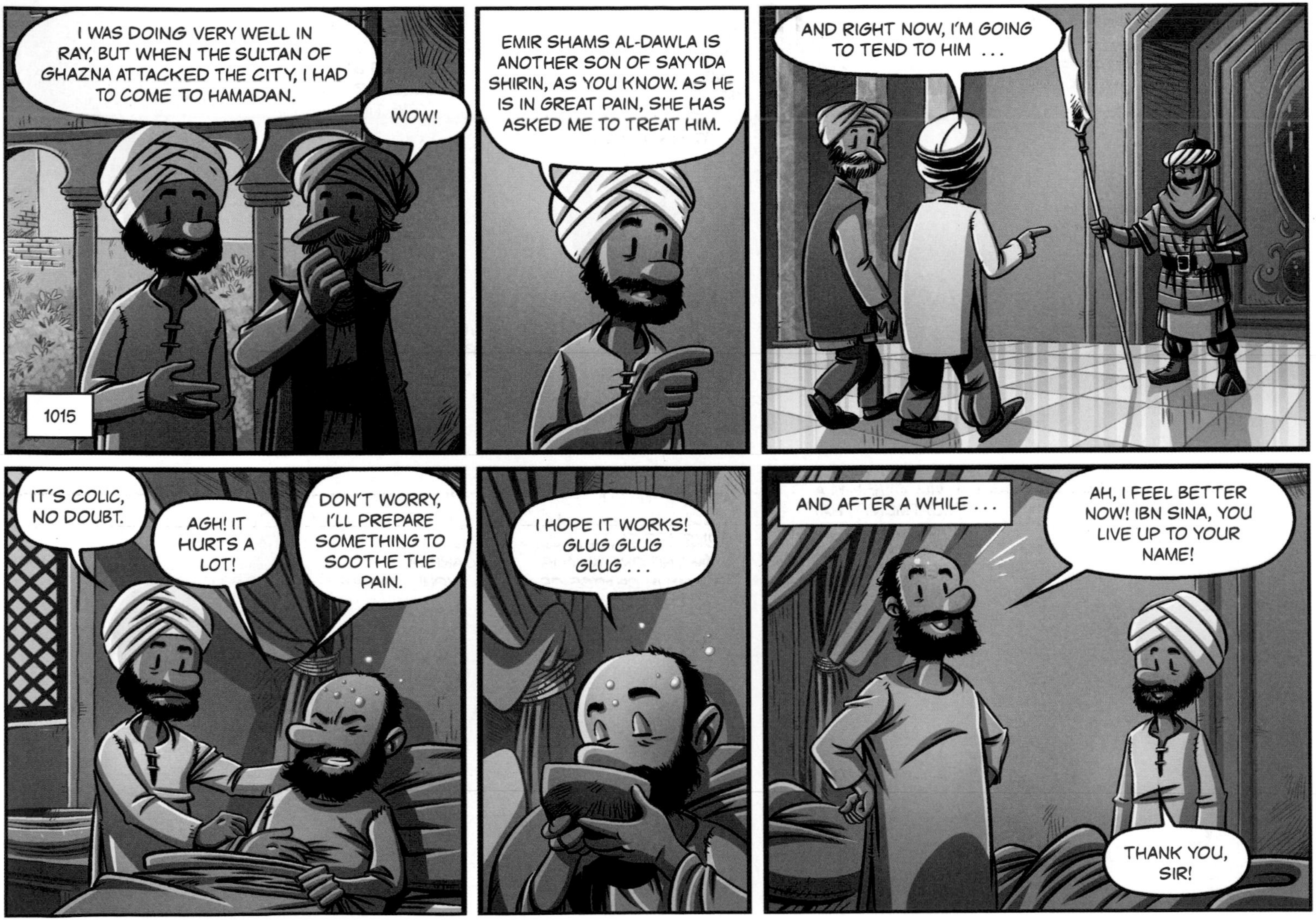
I WAS DOING VERY WELL IN RAY, BUT WHEN THE SULTAN OF GHAZNA ATTACKED THE CITY, I HAD TO COME TO HAMADAN.
WOW!
1015
EMIR SHAMS AL-DAWLA IS ANOTHER SON OF SAYYIDA SHIRIN, AS YOU KNOW. AS HE IS IN GREAT PAIN, SHE HAS ASKED ME TO TREAT HIM.
AND RIGHT NOW, I'M GOING TO TEND TO HIM . . .
IT'S COLIC, NO DOUBT.
AGH! IT HURTS A LOT!
DON'T WORRY, I'LL PREPARE SOMETHING TO SOOTHE THE PAIN.
I HOPE IT WORKS! GLUG GLUG GLUG . . .
AND AFTER A WHILE . . .
AH, I FEEL BETTER NOW! IBN SINA, YOU LIVE UP TO YOUR NAME!
THANK YOU, SIR!

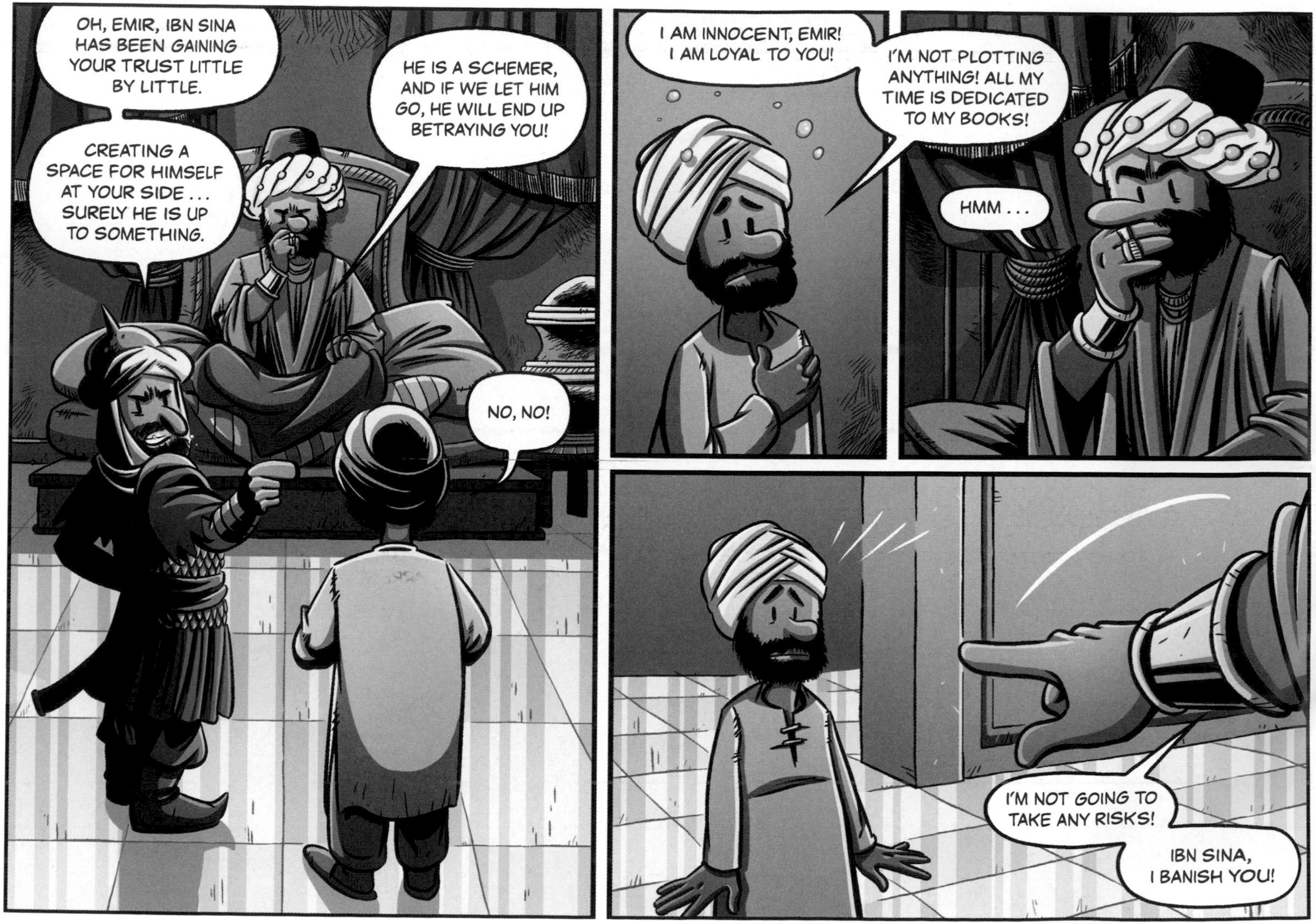
OH, EMIR, IBN SINA HAS BEEN GAINING YOUR TRUST LITTLE BY LITTLE.
CREATING A SPACE FOR HIMSELF AT YOUR SIDE . . . SURELY HE IS UP TO SOMETHING.
HE IS A SCHEMER, AND IF WE LET HIM GO, HE WILL END UP BETRAYING YOU!
NO, NO!
I AM INNOCENT, EMIR! I AM LOYAL TO YOU!
I'M NOT PLOTTING ANYTHING! ALL MY TIME IS DEDICATED TO MY BOOKS!
HMM . . .
I'M NOT GOING TO TAKE ANY RISKS!
IBN SINA, I BANISH YOU!

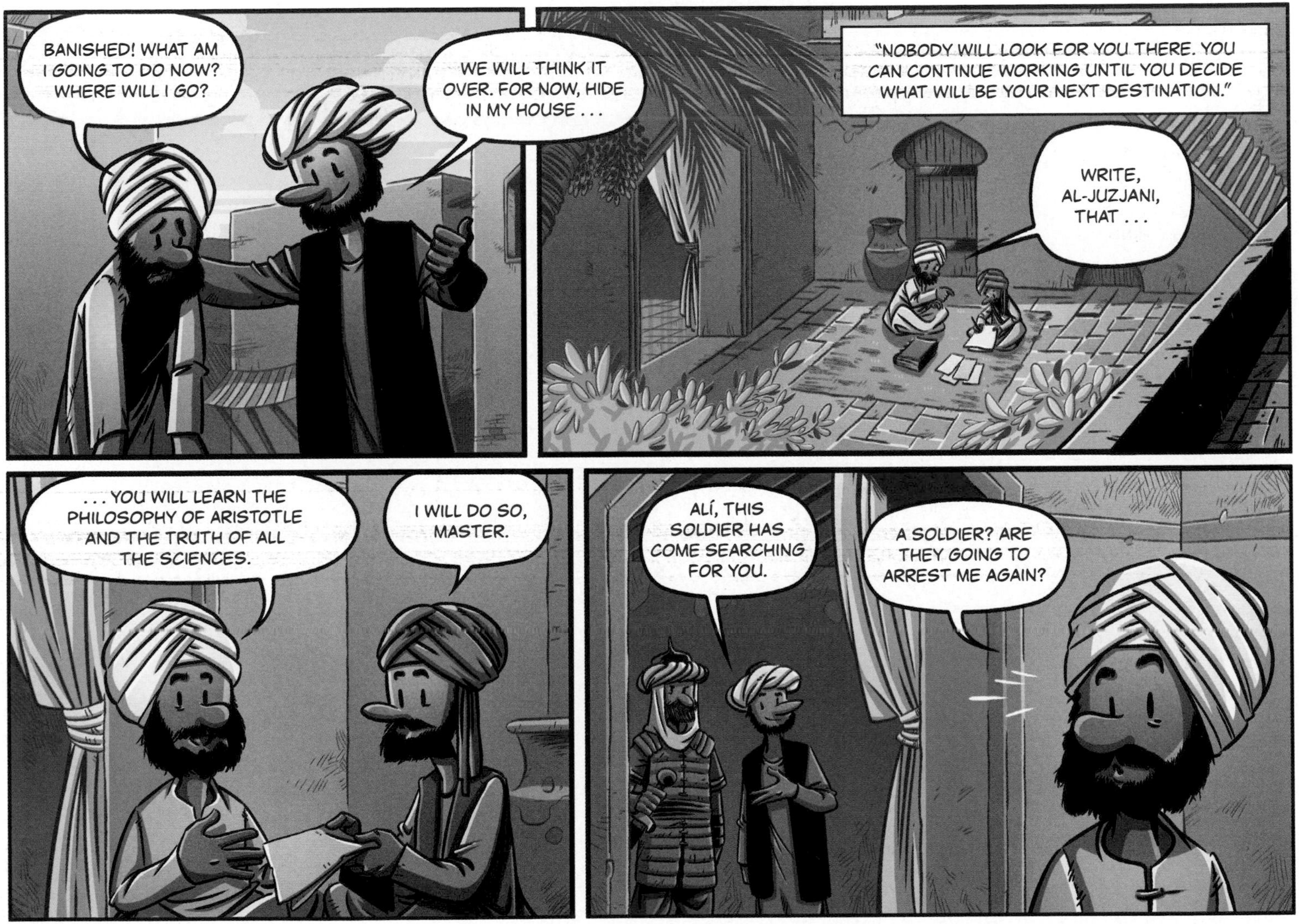
BANISHED! WHAT AM I GOING TO DO NOW? WHERE WILL I GO?
WE WILL THINK IT OVER. FOR NOW, HIDE IN MY HOUSE . . .
"NOBODY WILL LOOK FOR YOU THERE. YOU CAN CONTINUE WORKING UNTIL YOU DECIDE WHAT WILL BE YOUR NEXT DESTINATION."
WRITE, AL-JUZJANI, THAT . . .
. . . YOU WILL LEARN THE PHILOSOPHY OF ARISTOTLE AND THE TRUTH OF ALL THE SCIENCES.
I WILL DO SO, MASTER.
ALÍ, THIS SOLDIER HAS COME SEARCHING FOR YOU.
A SOLDIER? ARE THEY GOING TO ARREST ME AGAIN?

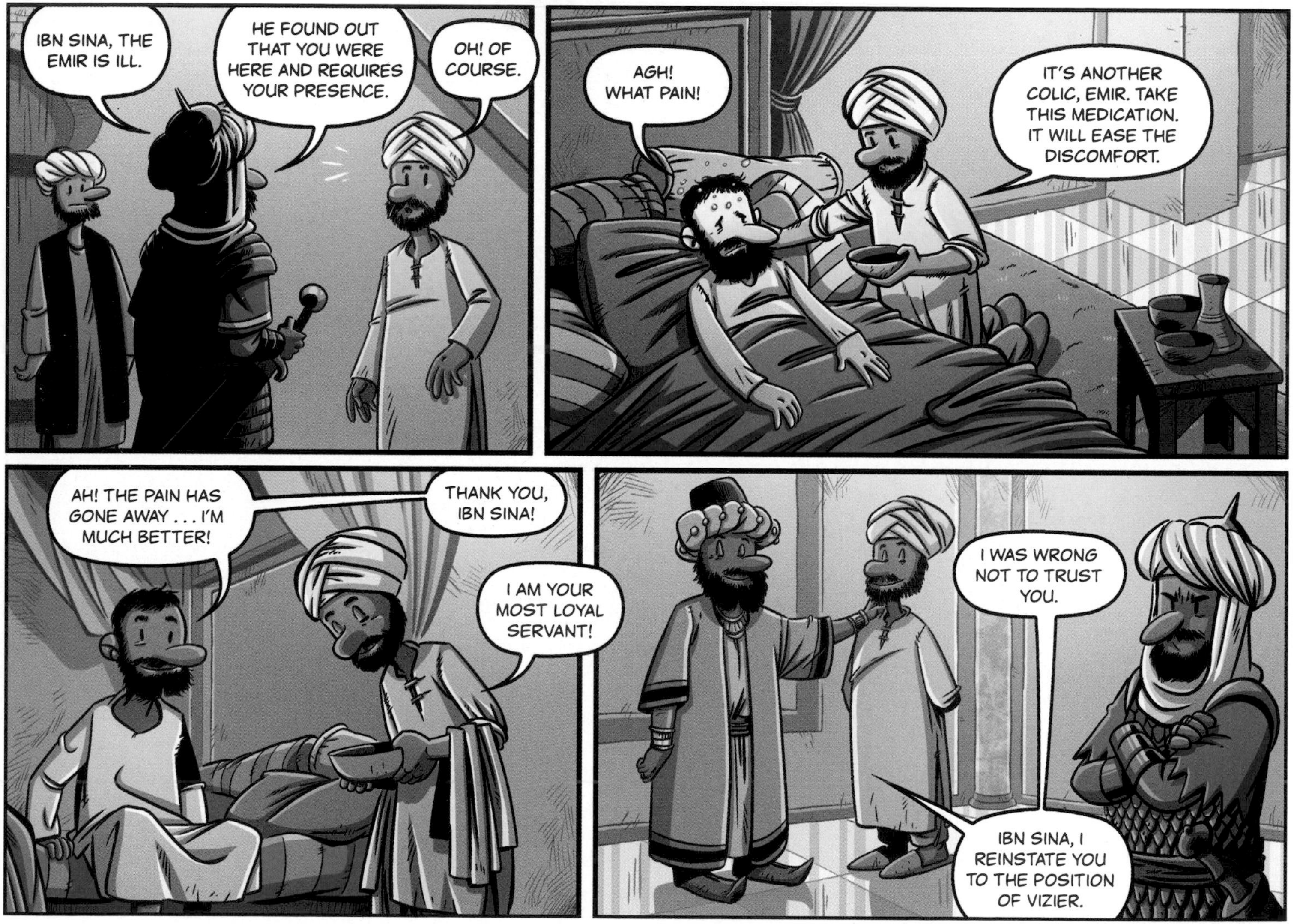
IBN SINA, THE EMIR IS ILL.
HE FOUND OUT THAT YOU WERE HERE AND REQUIRES YOUR PRESENCE.
OH! OF COURSE.
AGH! WHAT PAIN!
IT'S ANOTHER COLIC, EMIR. TAKE THIS MEDICATION. IT WILL EASE THE DISCOMFORT.
AH! THE PAIN HAS GONE AWAY . . . I'M MUCH BETTER!
THANK YOU, IBN SINA!
I AM YOUR MOST LOYAL SERVANT!
I WAS WRONG NOT TO TRUST YOU.
IBN SINA, I REINSTATE YOU TO THE POSITION OF VIZIER.

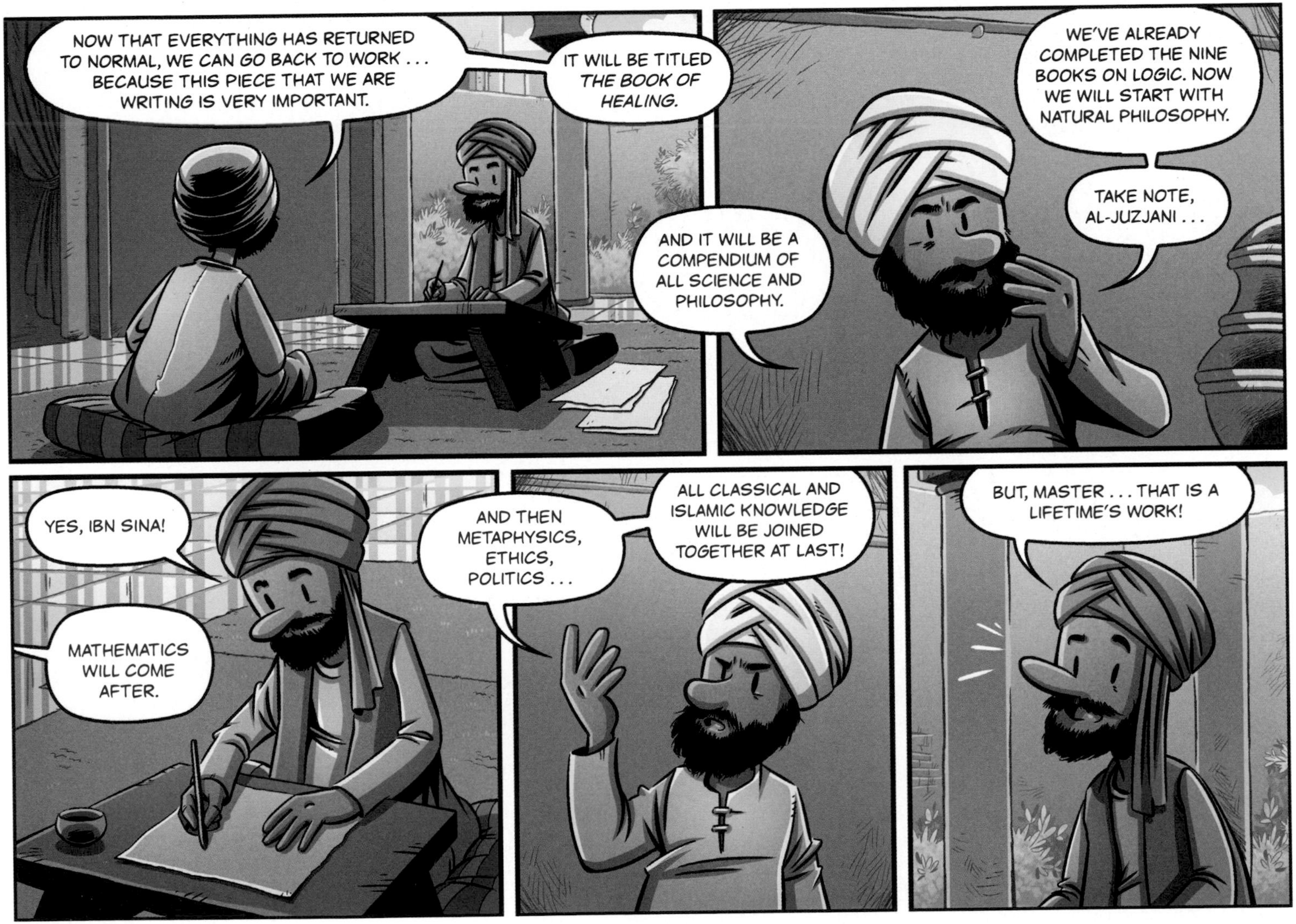
NOW THAT EVERYTHING HAS RETURNED TO NORMAL, WE CAN GO BACK TO WORK . . . BECAUSE THIS PIECE THAT WE ARE WRITING IS VERY IMPORTANT.
IT WILL BE TITLED *THE BOOK OF HEALING.*
AND IT WILL BE A COMPENDIUM OF ALL SCIENCE AND PHILOSOPHY.
WE'VE ALREADY COMPLETED THE NINE BOOKS ON LOGIC. NOW WE WILL START WITH NATURAL PHILOSOPHY.
TAKE NOTE, AL-JUZJANI . . .
YES, IBN SINA!
MATHEMATICS WILL COME AFTER.
AND THEN METAPHYSICS, ETHICS, POLITICS . . .
ALL CLASSICAL AND ISLAMIC KNOWLEDGE WILL BE JOINED TOGETHER AT LAST!
BUT, MASTER . . . THAT IS A LIFETIME'S WORK!

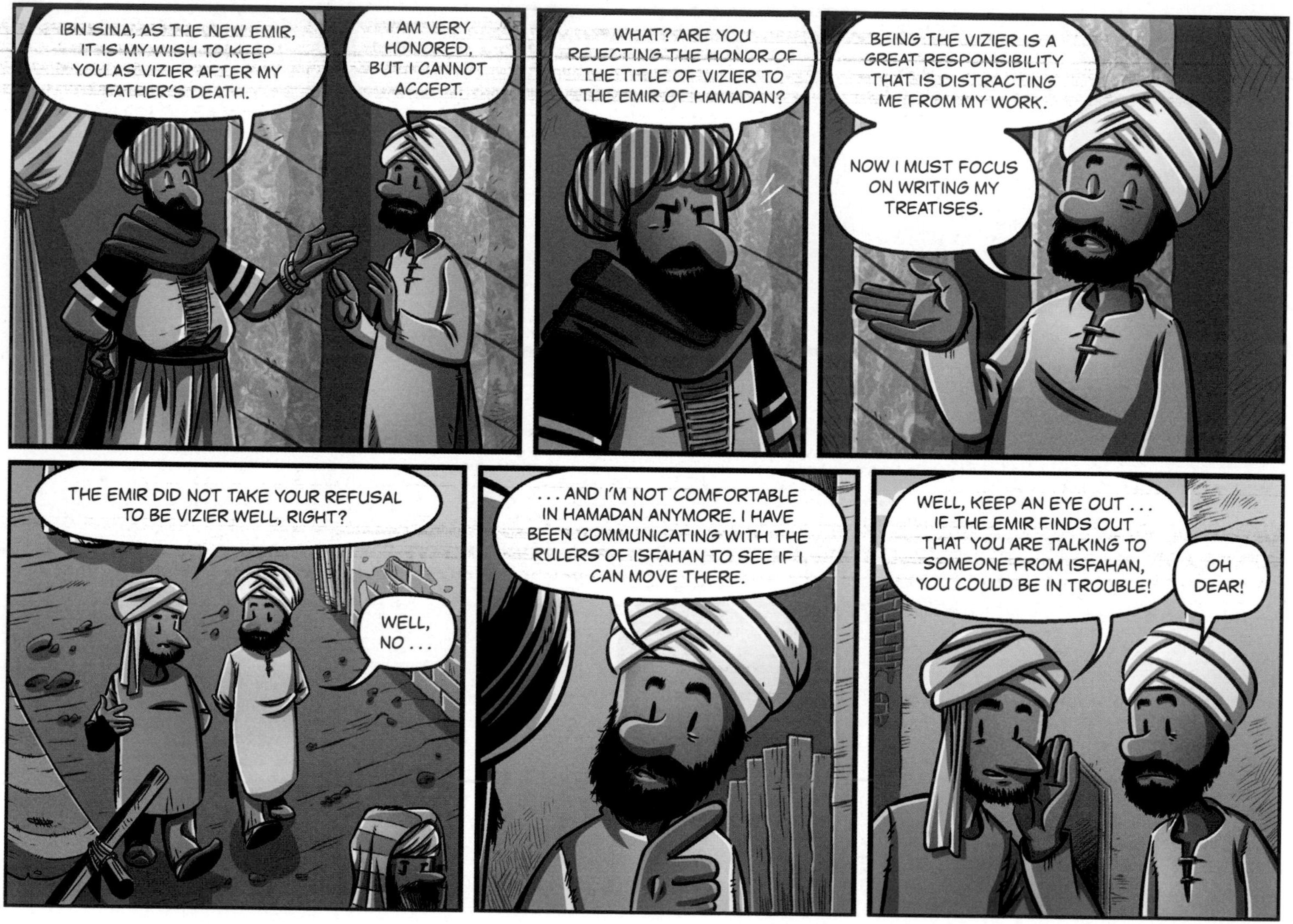
IBN SINA, AS THE NEW EMIR, IT IS MY WISH TO KEEP YOU AS VIZIER AFTER MY FATHER'S DEATH.
I AM VERY HONORED, BUT I CANNOT ACCEPT.
WHAT? ARE YOU REJECTING THE HONOR OF THE TITLE OF VIZIER TO THE EMIR OF HAMADAN?
BEING THE VIZIER IS A GREAT RESPONSIBILITY THAT IS DISTRACTING ME FROM MY WORK.
NOW I MUST FOCUS ON WRITING MY TREATISES.
THE EMIR DID NOT TAKE YOUR REFUSAL TO BE VIZIER WELL, RIGHT?
WELL, NO . . .
. . . AND I'M NOT COMFORTABLE IN HAMADAN ANYMORE. I HAVE BEEN COMMUNICATING WITH THE RULERS OF ISFAHAN TO SEE IF I CAN MOVE THERE.
WELL, KEEP AN EYE OUT . . . IF THE EMIR FINDS OUT THAT YOU ARE TALKING TO SOMEONE FROM ISFAHAN, YOU COULD BE IN TROUBLE!
OH DEAR!

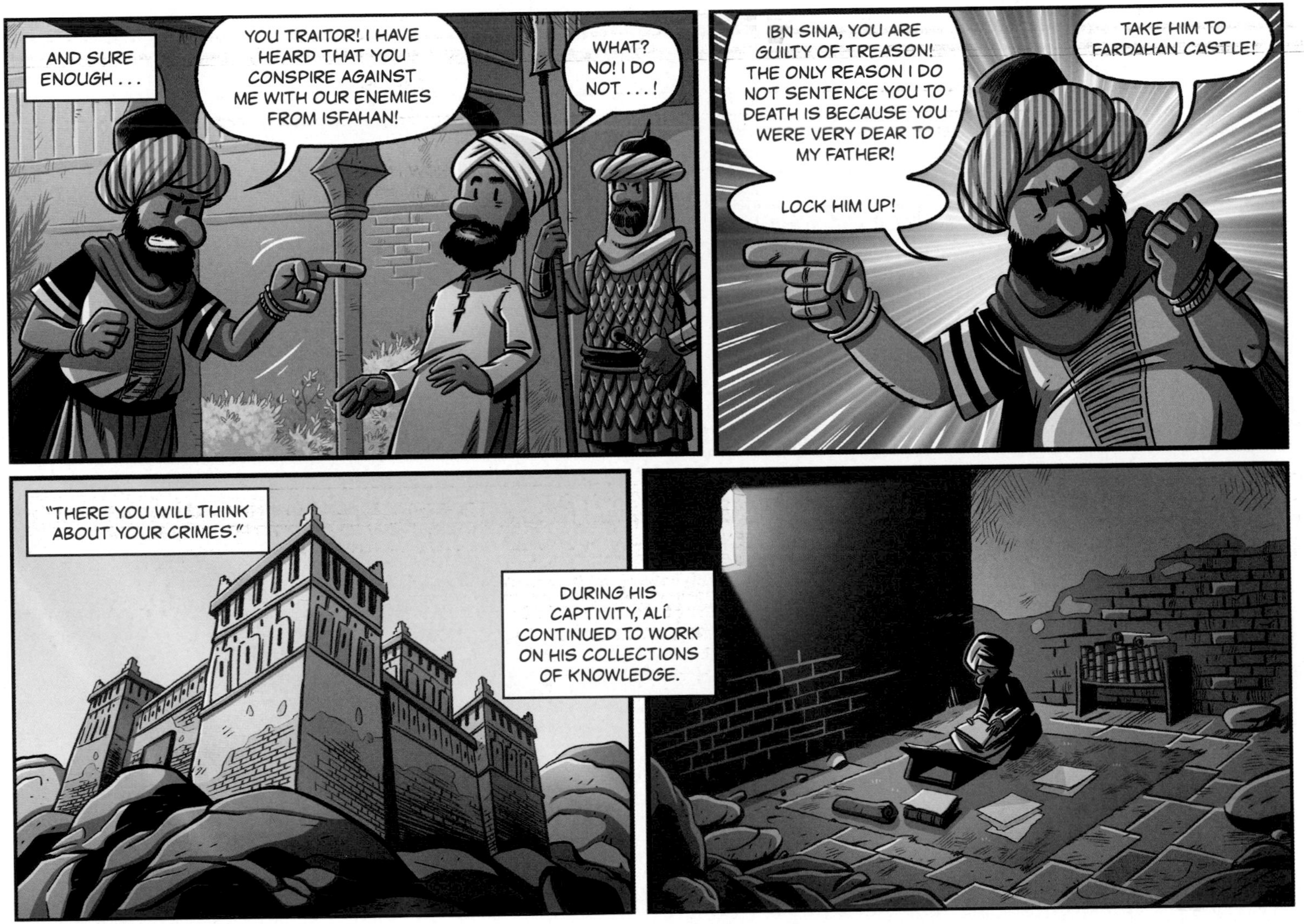
AND SURE ENOUGH . . .
YOU TRAITOR! I HAVE HEARD THAT YOU CONSPIRE AGAINST ME WITH OUR ENEMIES FROM ISFAHAN!
WHAT? NO! I DO NOT . . . !
IBN SINA, YOU ARE GUILTY OF TREASON! THE ONLY REASON I DO NOT SENTENCE YOU TO DEATH IS BECAUSE YOU WERE VERY DEAR TO MY FATHER!
LOCK HIM UP!
TAKE HIM TO FARDAHAN CASTLE!
"THERE YOU WILL THINK ABOUT YOUR CRIMES."
DURING HIS CAPTIVITY, ALÍ CONTINUED TO WORK ON HIS COLLECTIONS OF KNOWLEDGE.

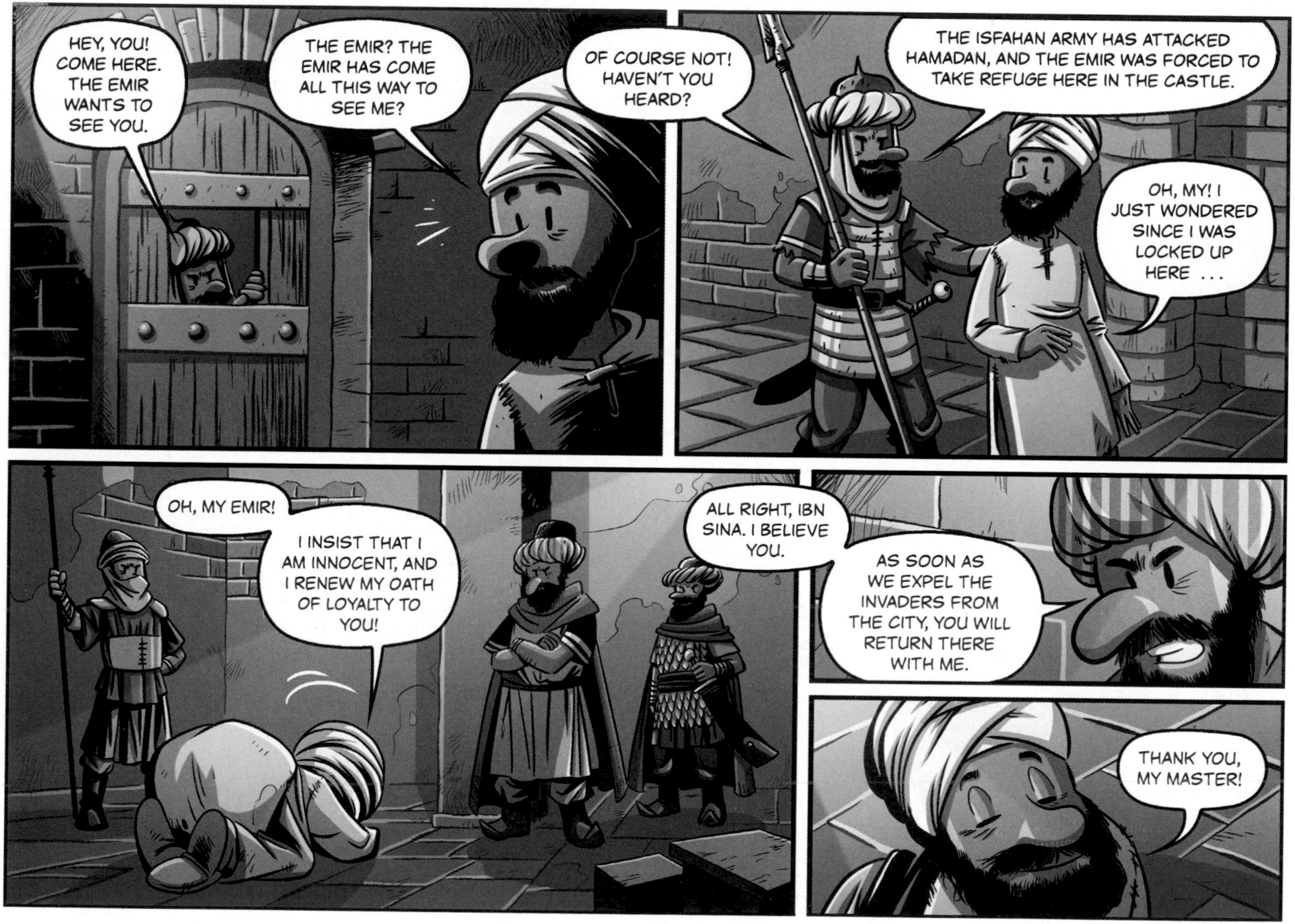
HEY, YOU! COME HERE. THE EMIR WANTS TO SEE YOU.
THE EMIR? THE EMIR HAS COME ALL THIS WAY TO SEE ME?
OF COURSE NOT! HAVEN'T YOU HEARD?
THE ISFAHAN ARMY HAS ATTACKED HAMADAN, AND THE EMIR WAS FORCED TO TAKE REFUGE HERE IN THE CASTLE.
OH, MY! I JUST WONDERED SINCE I WAS LOCKED UP HERE . . .
OH, MY EMIR!
I INSIST THAT I AM INNOCENT, AND I RENEW MY OATH OF LOYALTY TO YOU!
ALL RIGHT, IBN SINA. I BELIEVE YOU.
AS SOON AS WE EXPEL THE INVADERS FROM THE CITY, YOU WILL RETURN THERE WITH ME.
THANK YOU, MY MASTER!

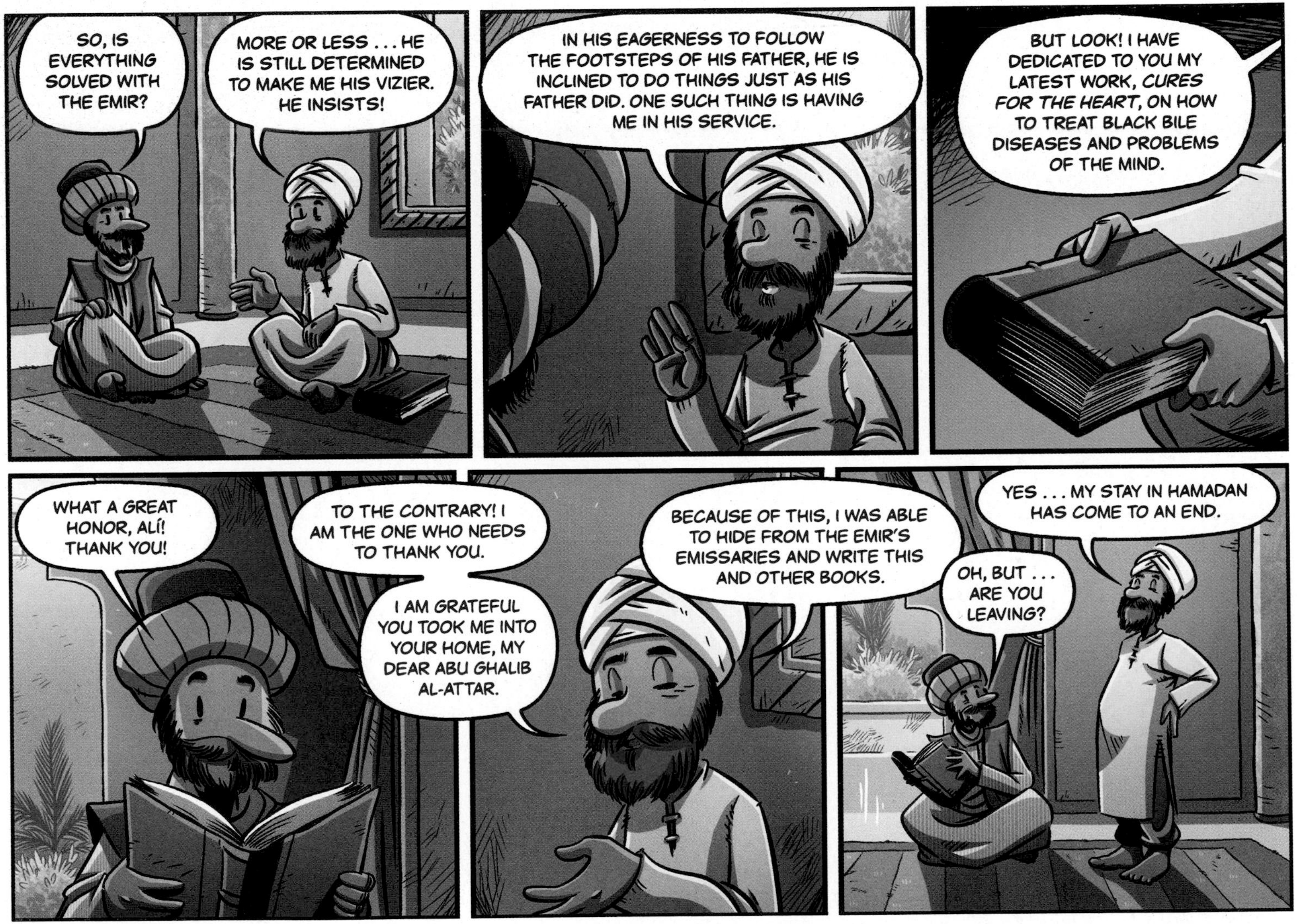
SO, IS EVERYTHING SOLVED WITH THE EMIR?
MORE OR LESS . . . HE IS STILL DETERMINED TO MAKE ME HIS VIZIER. HE INSISTS!
IN HIS EAGERNESS TO FOLLOW THE FOOTSTEPS OF HIS FATHER, HE IS INCLINED TO DO THINGS JUST AS HIS FATHER DID. ONE SUCH THING IS HAVING ME IN HIS SERVICE.
BUT LOOK! I HAVE DEDICATED TO YOU MY LATEST WORK, *CURES FOR THE HEART*, ON HOW TO TREAT BLACK BILE DISEASES AND PROBLEMS OF THE MIND.
WHAT A GREAT HONOR, ALÍ! THANK YOU!
TO THE CONTRARY! I AM THE ONE WHO NEEDS TO THANK YOU.
I AM GRATEFUL YOU TOOK ME INTO YOUR HOME, MY DEAR ABU GHALIB AL-ATTAR.
BECAUSE OF THIS, I WAS ABLE TO HIDE FROM THE EMIR'S EMISSARIES AND WRITE THIS AND OTHER BOOKS.
YES . . . MY STAY IN HAMADAN HAS COME TO AN END.
OH, BUT . . . ARE YOU LEAVING?

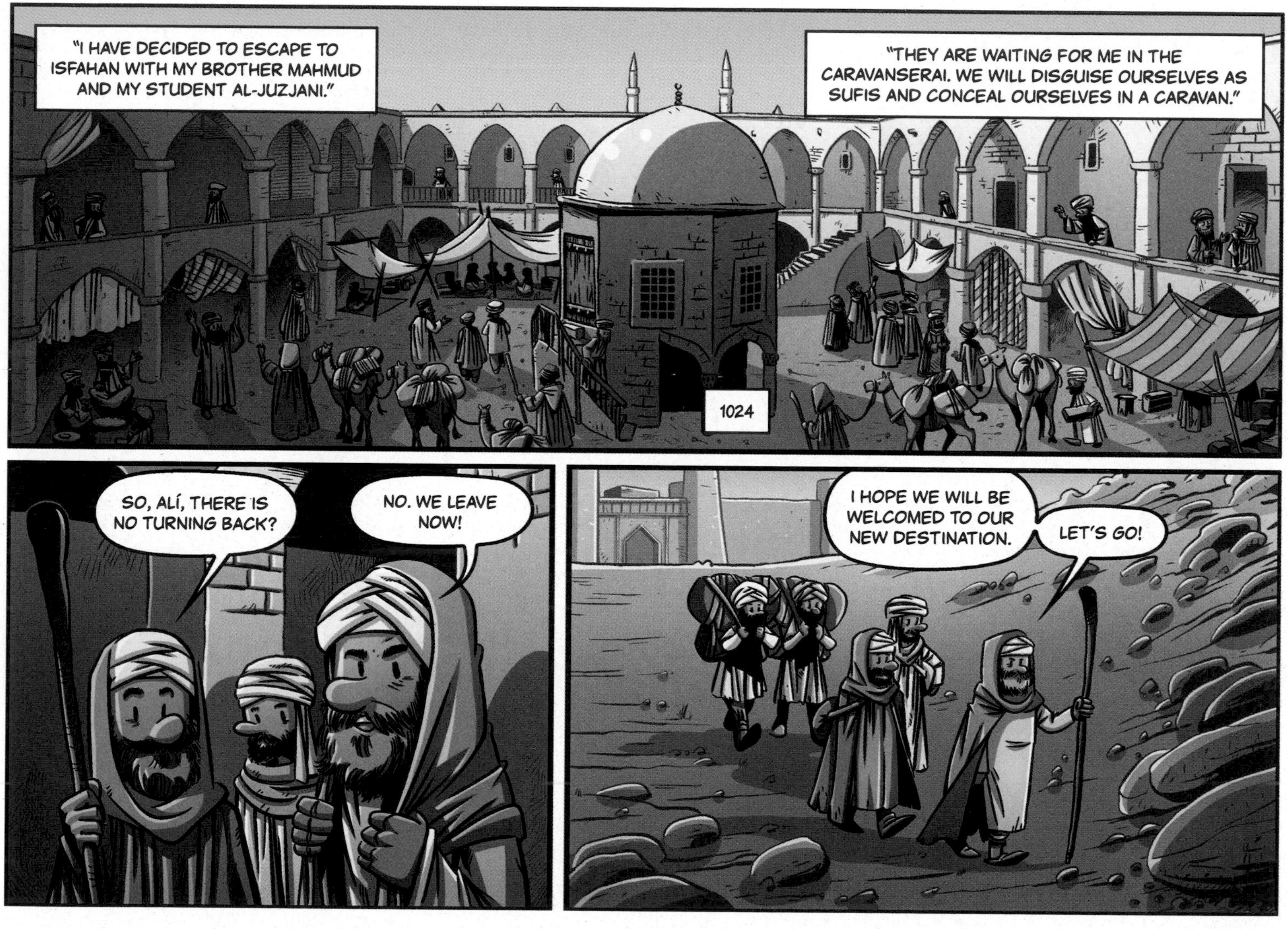
"I HAVE DECIDED TO ESCAPE TO ISFAHAN WITH MY BROTHER MAHMUD AND MY STUDENT AL-JUZJANI."
"THEY ARE WAITING FOR ME IN THE CARAVANSERAI. WE WILL DISGUISE OURSELVES AS SUFIS AND CONCEAL OURSELVES IN A CARAVAN."
1024
SO, ALÍ, THERE IS NO TURNING BACK?
NO. WE LEAVE NOW!
I HOPE WE WILL BE WELCOMED TO OUR NEW DESTINATION.
LET'S GO!

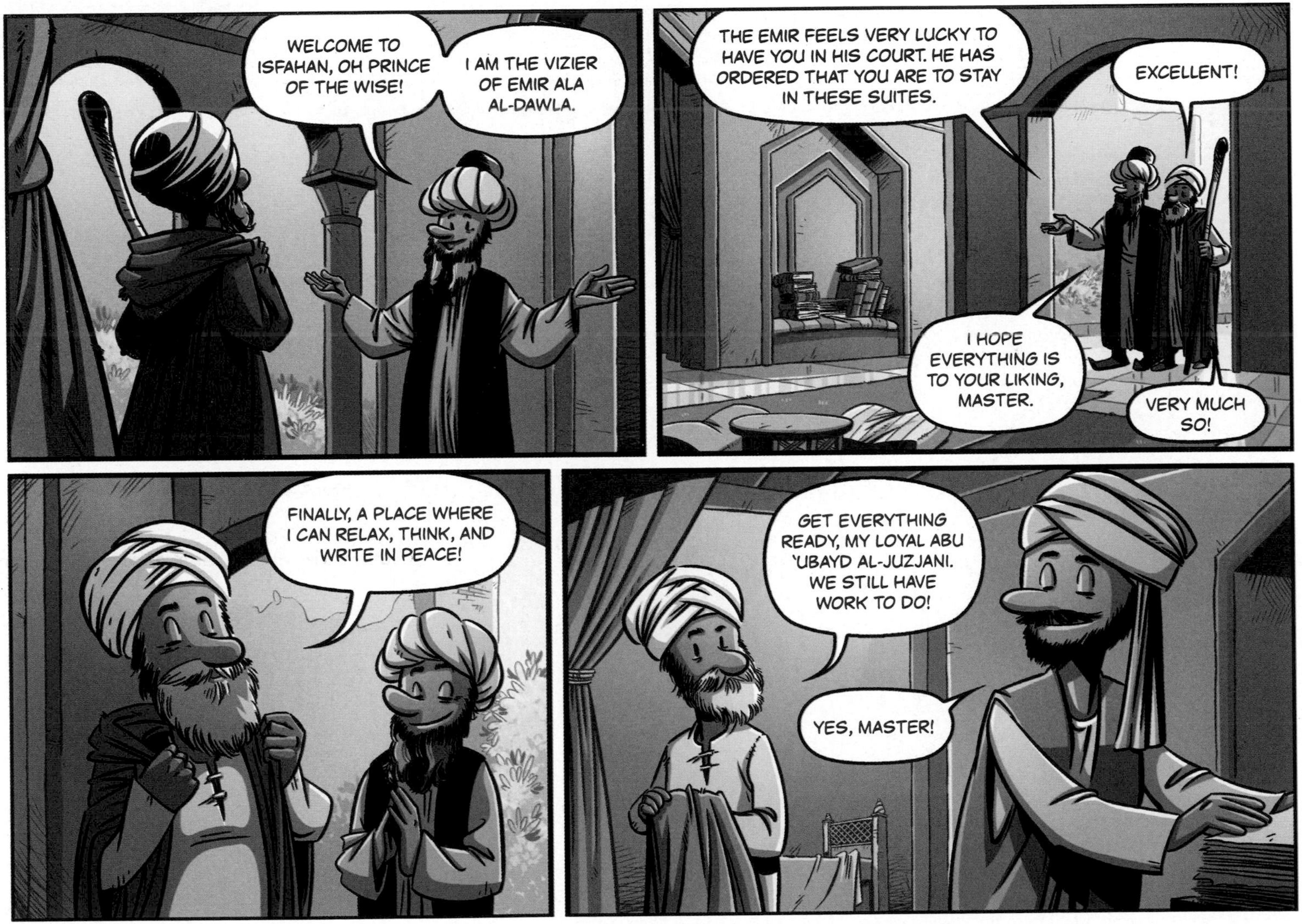
WELCOME TO ISFAHAN, OH PRINCE OF THE WISE!
I AM THE VIZIER OF EMIR ALA AL-DAWLA.
THE EMIR FEELS VERY LUCKY TO HAVE YOU IN HIS COURT. HE HAS ORDERED THAT YOU ARE TO STAY IN THESE SUITES.
EXCELLENT!
I HOPE EVERYTHING IS TO YOUR LIKING, MASTER.
VERY MUCH SO!
FINALLY, A PLACE WHERE I CAN RELAX, THINK, AND WRITE IN PEACE!
GET EVERYTHING READY, MY LOYAL ABU 'UBAYD AL-JUZJANI. WE STILL HAVE WORK TO DO!
YES, MASTER!

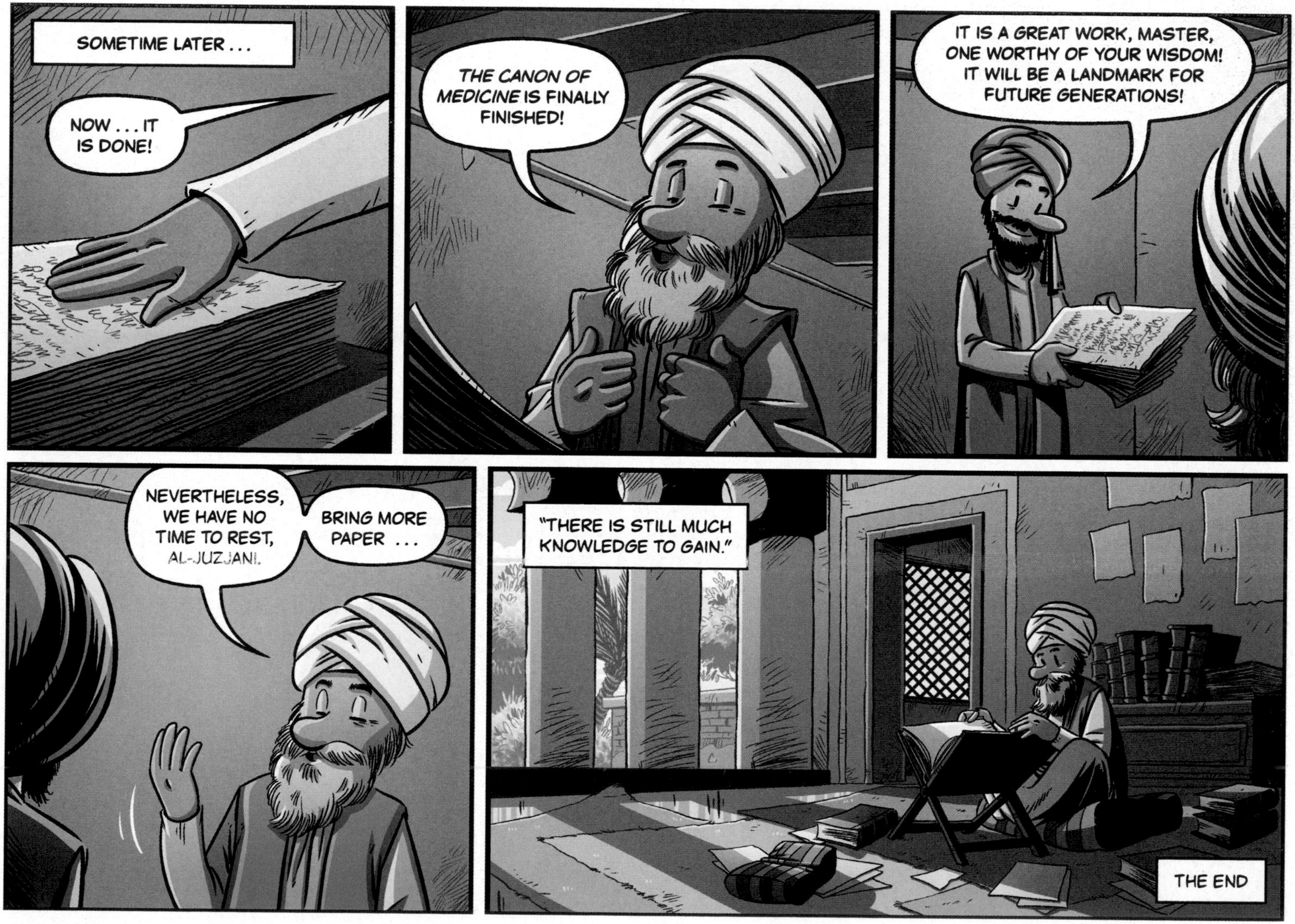
SOMETIME LATER . . .
NOW . . . IT IS DONE!
THE CANON OF MEDICINE IS FINALLY FINISHED!
IT IS A GREAT WORK, MASTER, ONE WORTHY OF YOUR WISDOM! IT WILL BE A LANDMARK FOR FUTURE GENERATIONS!
NEVERTHELESS, WE HAVE NO TIME TO REST, AL-JUZJANI.
BRING MORE PAPER . . .
"THERE IS STILL MUCH KNOWLEDGE TO GAIN."
THE END

TIMELINE

980: Ibn Sina, also known as Avicenna, is born in the Persian village of Afshana (in modern Uzbekistan).

997: In Bukhara, he becomes a physician to a local ruler.

999: He moves to Gurganj and enters the service of Emir Ibn Mamun.

1012: He leaves for the village of Jurjan. There, he stays in the home of a patron and meets his pupil Abu 'Ubayd al-Juzjani.

1014: In the city of Ray, he enters the service of Emir Majd al-Dawla and his mother, Sayyida Shirin.

1015: He travels to Hamadan after the sultan of Ghazna attacks Ray.

1021: He goes into hiding with patron Abu Ghalib al-Attar after pressure to become the vizier to Shams al-Dawla against his wishes. Around this time, he completes *The Book of Healing*, a scientific and philosophical encyclopedia.

1024: He relocates to Isfahan and the court of Emir Ala al-Dawla.

1025: He completes *The Canon of Medicine*, a collection of Islamic medical knowledge and its influences.

1037: He dies in Hamadan on June 22, following a severe colic.

GLOSSARY

ASTRONOMY: the area of natural science that studies space and celestial objects

BILE: a bitter fluid inside the body that aids digestion

CALIPH: a Muslim civil and religious ruler

CALIPHATE: the reign of a caliph or the area over which a caliph rules

CLASSICAL: related to ancient Greek philosophy or culture

COLIC: abdominal pain caused by gas or blockage of an intestine

CURRICULUM: the subjects that make up a course of study

DYNASTY: a line of rulers over time, usually within the same family

EMIR: a local Muslim ruler, sometimes a military leader

FITNA: an uprising or civil war

HUMORS: liquid elements that early medical texts suggested form the essence of the human body

IMAM: a religious leader, often a leader of prayer

ISLAMIC: related to the religion of Islam

ISMA'ILISM: a branch of Shia Islam

MISSIONARY: a person sent on a religious mission or journey

MOSQUE: a Muslim place of worship

PATRON: a person who gives support to people or causes

VIZIER: an official or adviser

FURTHER RESOURCES

"10 Facts about Ibn Sina"
    https://youtu.be/ngytVJv0Juw

"Ibn Sina's *The Canon of Medicine*"
    https://youtu.be/iM7NEfhTbno

Mann, Dionna L. *Hidden Heroes in Medicine*. Minneapolis: Lerner Publications, 2022.

Terrell, Brandon. *The Discovery of Germs*. Minneapolis: Graphic Universe, 2022.

INDEX